Meaningful Art Education

"Zebras." Brush drawing by an eleven-year-old boy.

MEANINGFUL
ART EDUCATION

By MILDRED M. LANDIS

Dual Professor of Art and Education
Syracuse University, Syracuse, N. Y.

Chas. A. Bennett Co., Inc. PUBLISHERS
PEORIA, ILLINOIS

PREFACE

A constant flow of ideas is generated and explored in each opportunity for creative expression. Creative ideas grow and achieve deeper meaning in the degree to which they are intelligently evaluated. Those of us who are teaching art in the schools are apt to rely too much on "instinct" in evaluating the art experience of the child. Creative expression is so complex in its nature that it deserves more than casual study if we are to make it integral in learning.

Within the last five years there has been some very valuable writing in both the philosophy and the psychology of art education. Inevitably there have been any number of books on techniques and the more mechanical aspects of teaching art in the school. While several outstanding statements have been made in the curriculum guides of a number of cities, there has been a need for more information on the nature of creative expression as it is found in school typical learning situations.

In MEANINGFUL ART EDUCATION Dr. Landis has provided material of great value to the development of art experiences in terms of the growth and developmental learning of the child.

Meaningful experiences in art for the growing child do not happen accidentally, Usually they follow the natural interests and needs of the child but as he grows it is important that teachers understand the goals and purposes for which art in the school is conceived. Art practices may be found which are based on tradition, whim, personal interest, or on something more intelligent.

As art educators we rely too much on time-worn statements of the value of creative expression in the education of the child. A little re-examination would help.

Are the art experiences we encourage for the child extensions of the realities or the physical and political world which point up the needs of individual groups in our society? Does our art education draw upon the facts of learning and growth that highlight human needs and suggest effective ways of meeting them? As one follows the approach to art education which Dr. Landis develops for us, one sees the real value of art experience in education. Her treatment deals objectively with children's art in terms long needed in general education.

An artist-teacher might feel that the motivating force in a child's creativity should be the desire to complete a product. As art educators we, with Dr. Landis, recognize that the development of the child is evaluated with the quality of the product. Teachers in typical school situations cannot give too much study to the creative processes which contribute to the whole growth of the child in interaction with all his learning experiences. Art should serve to clarify, stimulate, and extend the learning of the child.

MEANINGFUL ART EDUCATION should serve to help educators generally to realize the many ways in which a child may experience art at different levels of development in the school. This book should help further define the purposes of art education and extend the thinking of art educators in terms of larger aims.

IVAN E. JOHNSON
Consultant in Art Education
Dallas Public Schools

In Acknowledgment. I am particularly indebted to Professor Robert Ulich, who gave much help in the preparation of this book. I also wish to express my grateful appreciation to friends and students who gave helpful criticism. Many thanks are due the publishers of authorities quoted and to the Museum of Modern Art, who permitted me to use copyrighted material.

Mildred M. Landis.

Contents

PART TWO.   Classroom Applications

CHAPTER I

Four Approaches to Art Education

ART EDUCATION, if it is to be considered worthy
of a place in the elementary school curriculum, must
justify its position in terms of its broad educational
value. A narrow concept is likely to exclude the social
worth of that field to the extent that it also excludes
its right to social support. Art conceived as a mere
practice designed solely to occupy the otherwise idle
moments of the individual has little place in an educational system concerned with social values. Procedures, therefore, must be based on sound principles
of education; practices must be examined in terms of
their philosophical, psychological, and sociological importance. In other words, a practical plan must be
formulated that considers the nature of art as a process and a product, the value of art and art expression
to the individual, and the value of art to society.

Three main methods of art education may be widely observed in classroom practice today. These are defined here as a Directing method, a Free-expression method, and an Eclectic method. A fourth method, a Meaningful method, is beginning to appear. It is my purpose to set forth the principles of this method.

The term "directing method" is substituted here for the commonly used term "academic method" which is described by Dow in *A Cyclopedia of Education*.

"The academic method is truly analytic, teaching the pupils 'to see,' to gather fact upon fact, to store up knowledge to acquire skill. Its analogue is the old way of teaching language through grammar rather than through the use of language."[1]

The substitution of "directing" for "academic" is made here to differentiate between practices on the elementary school level and those on the higher level, which are more properly described by "academic." The necessity of this distinction is due to the kind of "subject matter" that has appeared in the elementary field, rather than to a basic difference in the method. The "analysis" which Dow mentions in the academic method was, for the most part, directed to the examination of classical and natural forms. On the elementary level, however, classical and natural forms have given way to a body of stereotyped patterns that more often than not have little resemblance to accurate visual forms nor to forms with any esthetic merit.

For the most part these patterns which are set up to be copied are commercial in origin. The presence of this material in elementary school practice seems to depreciate the meaning of academic.

THE DIRECTING METHOD

The Directing method represents that practice which requires the child to follow certain prescribed rules and directions. These have to do with measuring and making geometric designs; tracing around pattern figures; copying pictures from books, magazines, and teacher-drawn models; making accurate visual copies of leaves, flowers, or still-life groups; using color according to definite specifications; drawing according to principles of mechanical perspective. Absolute criteria of judgment are assumed to be possible in the Directing method; correct measurement, neatness, faithful visual reproduction of picture or object to be copied, definite color combinations, and accurate perspective are set up as standards of achievement. The *product* is of prime importance in this method and the nature of the product is predetermined by the teacher.

THE "FREE-EXPRESSION" METHOD

"Free-expression" is used here to describe a practice essentially opposite the Directing method. As this term is commonly used, it is subject to much loose interpretation. Sometimes another term quite as loosely interpreted, the term "self-expression" is substituted.

Either of these terms may refer on the one hand to a complete lack of either internal or external organization or, if emphasis is placed on the right-hand side of the hyphen — on expression, a considerable degree of meaning and order may be implied. For purposes of analysis here, the term will refer to practices that appear to be concerned with neither external nor internal control. At the same time, the less extreme meaning that the term is sometimes given is recognized.

The Free-expression method, then, instead of setting forth definite tasks to be accomplished, as does the Directing method, allows a maximum of freedom. Choice of subject, materials, and ways of using materials is entirely in the hands of the child. There are no particular standards to be met as far as the product is concerned. It matters little what the child produces as long as he is happy in his work. The *process* rather than the *product* is emphasized in the Free-expression method.

THE ECLECTIC METHOD

The third or Eclectic method is an attempt to compromise between the Directing and the Free-expression methods. Here a certain amount of freedom is allowed; but that freedom is interspersed with definite directions, in the hope that skills and techniques may be developed along with expression. This method might more properly be considered as a variation of either

the Directing or the Free-expression methods, inas-
much as any logical integration of these opposing methods is impossible. The Eclectic method finds no com-
patability of the two methods it includes. At times in
the Eclectic method practice will lean strongly toward
rigid direction, and at other times toward Free-
expression. The educational value of all three of these
methods is questioned.

CRITICISM OF DIRECTING METHOD

The Directing method is criticized by Thomas
Munro, who at the same time excuses its early existence as a necessary means of introducing art education into the schools. In *Art and Education,* by Dewey,
Barnes, and others, he states:

"A future historian may perhaps look tolerantly on
the shortcomings of the early stage in American school
art work. Its leaders had a difficult task in gaining
for art any recognition at all in the curriculum, against
the vigorous protest of hard-headed farmers and busi-
ness men, who thought anything beside the three R's
a wasteful indulgence in frills and fancies. If admitted
at all, it had always to conform to popular standards.
Thus picture-study was made a vehicle for patriotic
and moral lessons; drawing and painting consisted in
trying to reproduce a box in true perspective, or a
spray of flowers in pretty tints. Most teachers, of course,
were almost totally untrained either in the technique

or appreciation of art; they were few and overworked; hence their methods had to be capable of easy, standardized application to large classes, with clear-cut standards for grading results. Books of motives for decorative pattern were given out to them, simple stereotyped lotus-flowers, fleurs-de-lis and other conventional forms. Minute directions were prescribed for conducting an art class; in some cases, for example, each child was to have a sheet of paper printed with dots, and move his pencil in unison with the rest, three dots to the right, two down, and so on until a cat or house was outlined."[2]

Such procedures as are described above reduce art to little more than a mechanical skill. Under such procedures children do not and cannot use art as a means of expression. Drawing becomes a kind of practice for the few who persist under such methods; for the others (as the excuse is often given), "something for which they have no talent anyway."

The Free-expression method is also criticized. This method frequently becomes a reaction against the Directing practices.

CRITICISM OF FREE-EXPRESSION METHOD

The theory of free expression assumed that an individual might express himself entirely unaffected either by teacher or immediate environmental influence. This, according to Thomas Munro, is not possible:

"...the ideal of keeping a child's imagination in a state of absolute purity and freedom is from the start impossible. The very attempt at such an end is evidence of the false psychology which has affected much writing on art education: of the old belief that some 'self' within the child is bursting for expression and release, and that all outside forces tend to repress and enslave it.

"Yet the persistent attempt to shut out influence is sure to have some effect. For which types of art are easiest to keep away? Not the vulgar of the street nor the childish type of the school-room, but the great traditions of the past and the best works of the present. Not readily accessible, less ostentatious than the visible clamor around, buried in frozen disorder in museums, good works of art may never catch the child's attention or be understood, unless the teacher points them out, and invites him to see how they differ from things of more obvious appeal. Failure to do this can have only one result; that the bad influences have practically no competition."[3]

Professor Franz Cizek in his school in Vienna in the early twenties was the outstanding champion of the so-called Free-expression method. He is said to have been perfectly sincere in his belief that the work of his pupils was entirely free from outside influence. According to Thomas Munro, however, an examination of the work reveals a typical Cizek style and a great similarity between the work of different pupils, indicating that influence was exerted, although probably not deliberately or consciously, by Professor Cizek.

Under the Free-expression method, even where a certain amount of unconscious influence is exerted as seemed to be the case in the Cizek school, children become discouraged and soon lose interest in their art work. Dewey points out this tendency. In *Art and Education* he states:

"Revolt from the costly nerve-taxing and inadequate results of mechanical control from without creates an enthusiasm for spontaneity and 'development from within' as it is often phrased. It is found that children at first are then much happier in their work — anyone who has seen Cizek's class will testify to the wholesome air of cheerfulness, even of joy, which pervades the room — but gradually tend to become listless and finally bored, while there is an absence of cumulative progressive development of power and actual achievement in results."[4]

CRITICISM OF ECLECTIC METHOD

Recognition of the inadequacy of the two extremes of Direction and Free-expression is frequently followed by an attempt to compromise between the two, as in the Eclectic method. Such attempts usually meet with little success, for both the imitative and Free-expression practices lack a most essential element for effective education — *purpose on the part of the child*. The

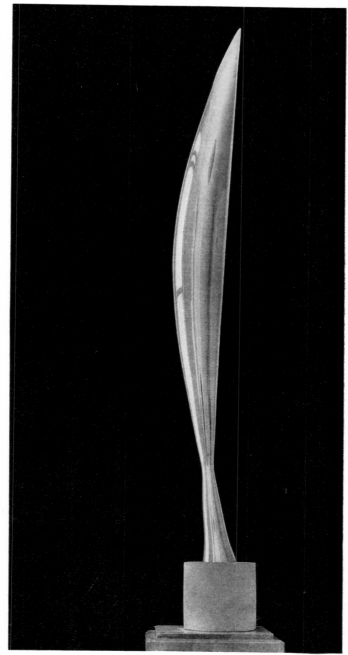

1. "Bird in Space," Brancusi. (Referred to on page 47.)

mere combining of two methods lacking *purpose* may hardly be expected to provide this essential element.

Dewey recognizes the fallacy of attempting to compromise between two faulty extremes. It is rather a change in direction that is necessary, he asserts:

"Unfortunately, the history of schools not only in art but in all lines shows a swing of the pendulum between two extremes, though it must be admitted that the simile of the pendulum is not a good one, for the schools remain, most of them, most of the time, near one extreme, instead of swinging periodically and evenly between the two. . . .

"The metaphor of the pendulum is faulty in another respect. It seems to suggest that the solution lies in finding a mid-point between the two extremes which would be at rest. But what is really wanted is a change in direction of movement."[5]

Learning, according to this "new direction," says Dewey, is controlled by two great principles: "One is participation in something inherently worthwhile, or undertaken on its own account; the other is perception of the relation of means to consequences. When these two conditions are met, a third condition usually follows as a matter of course. Having had an experience of the meaning of certain technical processes and forms of skill there develops an interest in skill and 'technique': the meaning of the result is 'transferred' to the means of its attainment."[6]

MEANINGFUL ART EDUCATION

Meaningful art education is concerned with this "new direction." The underlying principles of this fourth possible approach to art education, (1) that purpose is essential and (2) that there be some "relation of means to consequences," are not new to general educational theory. In regard to art education, however, there remains much to be done by way of developing a working plan that encompasses these principles.

Ulich in *Conditions of Civilized Living* emphasizes the importance of *purpose* in education: "...it is the close attachment to a definite purpose which enables an individual to become an integrated personality. The process of maturation, which is the molding of an individual into a well-operating whole, must not be understood as resulting from a mere mechanical balance of different faculties. Rather it needs a high degree of motivation to bend all the centrifugal powers in the human personality into a somewhat stable form. And this motivation is impossible without a purpose."[7]

Burton in *The Guidance of Learning Activities* states that there is no learning without purpose. He also points out the importance of the relation of means to end: "Learning does not take place without interest of some sort in the process and outcome....The problem is not whether children are to learn with interest or without it. They *never* learn without it."[8]

The report of the Harvard Committee emphasizes that *means* and *end* are inseparable in education: "Education can therefore be wholly devoted neither to tradition nor to experiment, neither to the belief that the ideal in itself is enough nor to the view that means are valuable apart from the ideal. It must uphold at the same time tradition and experiment, the ideal and the means, subserving, like our culture itself, change within commitment."[9]

To repeat, these principles are not new in general educational theory, but in art education there is considerable need to develop them in practice.

Meaningful art education is concerned with *purpose on the part of the individual* and the *relation of means to end,* process and product, and may not, like the Directing method, set up absolute rules of criteria of judgment; neither may such a method allow for complete "freedom." Rather it must foster the development of a "sense of values" — values that are concerned with esthetics, with the individual, and with society. "Purpose," or as Dewey terms it, "participation in something inherently worthwhile," is concerned with esthetic, psychological, and sociological *values.* Purpose linked with the necessity of a unity of process and product, means and end, must be based on *values* that have their roots in experience and practice but which may venture beyond the world of fact.

Art education that would avoid the extremes of

rigid direction and free expression must formulate
practices which help the individual develop a sense
of values, or an awareness of what Burton terms "persistent truths." For only through the development of
the ability to make value judgements is the individual
freed from slavish imitation on the one hand and aim-
less and often chaotic activity on the other. In other
words, he is freed from the extremes of absolutism and
relativism.

Burton discusses the problem of avoiding the extremes of relativism and absolutism and states the
necessity of finding principles that have been derived
from real life situations so often and over so long a
period of time that they are accepted as persistent
truths:

"It is as necessary to be on guard against the extremes of relativity as against the extremes of absolutism and authoritarianism. Many persons first meeting
the empirical theory of knowledge think that it rules
out ideals, standards of truth, love, beauty — rules out
so-called higher things which transcend earthbound
experience. Not at all. Empirical thinking goes beyond experience when it speculates upon what is
known, analyzes it, and imaginatively attempts to interpret and organize it. Liberal empiricism has ample
place for hopes, dreams, aspirations toward better
men and better worlds; but these hopes and aspirations
are rooted in the facts of experience and not on fan-

tasy which mysteriously transcends, that is, defies facts."[10]

Green in *The Arts and the Art of Criticism* states that a sense of values must be formed on a wide frame of reference and that emotion and reflection are necessary to evaluation:

"Our evaluations are conditioned partly by the emotional intensity and vividness of particular experiences, and partly by a sense of their larger implications. The less reflective the agent, the more will his evaluations be determined by the poignancy of each immediate experience; the more thoughtful he is, the more he will tend to evaluate his experiences and their objects in a wider frame of reference; i.e., in terms of their more ultimate import for himself and his fellow men. Both emotion and reflection are requisite to adequate evaluation. One of H. G. Wells' fantastic creatures from Mars, endowed with reason but devoid of all capacity for emotive response, could attach no greater significance to one experience than to another, and would regard all objects and events as equally devoid of import. A pure sentimentalist in contrast, indulges in unrestrained emotional response to the most unconsequential occurrence and fails to sense the import of occurrences to which more thoughtful individuals rightly attach great significance.

"Emotion and reflection are thus the chief subjective factors in human evaluation. Each individual's

synoptic sense of values, in turn may be termed his
'philosophy of life.' This philosophy of life is normally
not the product of professional philosophical inquiry."

Green concludes:

" 'The philosophy which is so important to each
of us,' says William James, 'is not a technical matter;
it is our more or less dumb sense of what life honestly
and deeply means. It is only partly got from books; it
is our individual way of just seeing and feeling the
total push and pressure of the cosmos.' "[11]

SUMMARY

A Directing method does not allow the individual
sufficient freedom necessary to the formulation or the
realization of a *purpose*. Lacking such a purpose the
individual cannot relate means to end. Under rigid
direction there is no place for the emotion or reflection necessary to the formation of a sense of values.

The Free-expression method without internal or
external control and characterized by many loose ends
does not encourage the individual to the formulation
or realization of a purpose without which there may
be no relation of means to end. Rather than emotion
there is *exhaustion of energy*; rather than reflection
there is *random activity*. A sense of values can result
from neither.

The Eclectic method, being a variation of the Directing and the Free-expression methods, has the dis-
advantages of each.

Meaningful art education is concerned with immediate as well as broad purpose, and with the unity of means and end. It allows the individual sufficient freedom for emotion and reflection. These factors accompanied by ever widening experience may enable the individual to develop a sense of values essential to art and living.

It is my purpose to develop such a method in terms of classroom practice, but before doing so it is well to examine underlying principles of esthetics. The customary art program is mainly concerned with suggestions of what the child may make, paint, or draw from day to day. Such a program disregards the traditional meaning of art as an important means of expression. For that reason it is essential to ask oneself, first, what are esthetic values? What differentiates a work of art from that which is not a work of art? Secondly, assuming that there are esthetic values, of what benefit may these be for the individual? Thirdly, what are some of the values of art creativity for society?

On the basis of the tentative answers to these questions, procedures which may help teachers guide school children to meaningful art creativity will be developed.

REFERENCE BOOKS, CHAPTER I

[1]*A Cyclopedia of Education,* Paul Monroe, Editor, New York: Macmillan Co., 1911. Vol. I, pp. 230-231.

[2]Dewey, John; Barnes, Albert C.; Buermeyer, Laurence; Munro, Thomas; and Others, *Art and Education.* Merion, Pa.: The Barnes Foundation Press, 1929. p. 330.

[3]*Ibid.,* Thomas Munro, "Franz Cizek and the Free Expression Method," pp. 314-315.

[4]*Ibid.,* John Dewey, "Individuality and Experience," pp. 175-176.

[5]*Ibid.,* pp. 175-176.

[6]*Ibid,* p. 177.

[7]Ulich, Robert, *Conditions of Civilized Living.* New York: E. P. Dutton and Co., Inc., 1946. p. 72.

[8]Burton, William H., *The Guidance of Learning Activities.* New York: D. Appleton-Century Co., 1944. pp. 100-101.

[9]The Harvard Committee, *General Education in a Free Society.* Cambridge, Mass.: Harvard University Press, 1945. p. 51.

[10]*Op. cit.,* Burton, William H., p. 73.

[11]Green, Theodore Meyer, *The Arts and the Art of Criticism.* Princeton, N. J.: Princeton University Press, 1940. pp. 462-463.

CHAPTER II

Esthetic Principles
Essential to a
Meaningful Art Education

To ATTEMPT to draw a sharp line between esthetic and non-esthetic values or to claim what is ultimately beautiful or absolutely ugly would be presumptuous indeed. But in spite of the lack of a definite criterion for evaluating visual art works, some basis for judgement of the relative value of one work over another is necessary in formulating a practical plan for art education.

Certainly every picture or piece of sculpture that happens to be made cannot lay claim to artistic or esthetic merit; otherwise, the realm of art would be chaotic and meaningless. There is a problem then to discover some essential qualities, some values that might serve as a basis of judgment and at the same time not limit art with dogmatic rules.

NON-ESTHETIC ELEMENTS

Painting, sculpture, architecture, and craft are liked for many different reasons, certainly not all of them esthetic ones. Some non-esthetic elements have strong human appeal and should be understood in their proper relationship to artistic values. Properly understood so-called non-esthetic qualities may serve as a vehicle to esthetic expression; if these qualities are not understood, but are confused with esthetic values, they may sabotage the whole art program by making art merely a form of practice with little artistic meaning or educational value.

Some of the qualities which easily tend to be extraneous to a real understanding of art are: *The story telling quality:* This seems to be the one with the most immediate appeal. The prevalence of picture magazines and tabloid newspapers now on the market attests to this.

Sentimental association: A work that serves as a reminder of some actual event may bring pleasure to the observer.

Object familiar to the observer: Forms that are familiar are liked, while new or strange forms may be considered ugly.

Isolated "skill": The difficulty that is overcome

in accomplishing a task sometimes evokes the admiration of the observer.

Monetary value: The work may have a high market value, and therefore be of interest to the spectator.

The label: "This is a Rembrandt," or "This is a Titian," may be all that is required to stimulate admiration of a painting.

Painting or other visual works may possess any or all of the above qualities, and, much as they may be liked or enjoyed for these qualities, may not be necessarily works of art in the esthetic sense.

The story telling quality, for example, may exist in a work of art, but it may also exist in a cheap billboard advertisement or in an inferior comic strip that no one would claim to be art. It would seem quite reasonable then to conclude that in isolation this element is a rather doubtful criterion for judgment of artistic merit. It is not so much *that* a story is told in paint or other media, as *how* a story is told in the media selected, that determines a work of art.

Sometimes because the subject matter of a story telling picture is taken from history or great literature, the issue for art is even more confused. The real esthetic quality of the event may exist in the other medium — that is, the written word, or the medium of literature — while the painting may serve only as a cue or a reminder of some esthetic experience due to the use of words and not to the use of paint. For example, a painting of Lucifer being cast into "bottom-less perdition" may serve to bring to mind a passage from Milton's *Paradise Lost*. The subject matter of the painting may bring to the observer's mind the literary passage. Once the cue is given, the esthetic enjoyment is of the literature, with the particular lines running through one's mind.

While there is no particular objection to such a relationship, there is an artistic objection, as pertains to the visual arts; for painting itself has within it the power to arouse the emotions that Milton's words arouse. Satan and his fallen angels might well be so painted that the magnitude and tragedy of their fall are fully expressed. In other words, paint, clay, and wood have their own expressive qualities and if properly used do not need to refer to another medium, namely words, before an idea is conveyed.

Sentimental association may also confuse judgement of painting or sculpture if the work serves only as a cue to some event quite apart from the enjoyment and contemplation of the painting itself. A painting of the "old homestead" may give great pleasure to the person who has lived there and may leave the person who has not, little moved. A simple glance at such a painting may be all that is required to cause one to relive the experience of a happy childhood. A bad photograph can do as much.

It is necessary to distinguish between *sentimental*

association, where the observer is completely detached from the art work and aware only of the object of reference, and association which does not separate the art work from the idea.

In *sentimental* association, more frequently than not, the observer leans so strongly toward the object of reference that the intrinsic elements of the painting lose all value. It is as though one likes a friend because he is like some other friend and not because he himself has desirable characteristics.

Music is a strong "conditioner" in the formulation of sentimental associations. A musical selection, good or bad, heard during a moment of emotional intensity, forever after brings to the mind of the listener the event of that moment.

The worst juke box blast can be associated with the first meeting of boy and girl and ever after be "the favorite song" for both of them.

Association, on the other hand, is essential to esthetic enjoyment. To claim otherwise is to deny that art should have meaning. Dewey emphasizes that association may not be separate from the art work; neither may the art work exist as separate from the association. The two, internally integrated, are necessary to an artistic or expressive object:

"But the truth of esthetic theory cannot be arrived at by a mechanical addition of one theory to the other. The expressiveness of the object of art is due to the

fact that it presents a thorough and complete interpenetration of the materials of undergoing and of
action, the latter including a reorganization of matter
brought with us from past experience. For, in the
interpenetration, the latter is material not added by
way of external association nor yet by way of super-
imposition upon sense qualities. The expressiveness of
the object is the report and celebration of the complete
fusion of what we undergo and what our activity of
attentive perception brings into what we receive by
means of the senses."[1]

Familiarity with the object may cloud one's sense
of artistic appreciation. Forms that are familiar are
liked; those which are not are adjudged ugly. This
attitude is particularly true in regard to architecture
and craft. For example, one would encounter little
opposition in constructing a building according to the
prevailing style, even though such a building possessed
few fine artistic or functional relationships. Some of
the simpler functional forms of modern architecture
and furniture may have a unity and organization that
is completely missed by the person who accepts only
what is familiar to him.

To go beyond the familiar requires an effort that
disturbs one's tranquility, for there is no guarantee
that the new will be better than the old. The recognition and acceptance of new values requires experience and the understanding of ever changing human

needs. The old must not be cast aside simply because
it is old; neither should it be preserved eternally for
the same reason. Creativity and appreciation should
be concerned with artistic values wherever they may
be found, and age *per se* is not essentially one of them.
Artistic values, on the other hand, are not likely to
spring forth spontaneously without regard for roots
or tradition. Human beings have lived before our
time, and they, too, have had sensitivity to the life
about them. What they have discovered cannot be
ignored, but neither should such discovery limit future
creativity. Great art works of the past were creations
of their time and this creativity must continue.

A display of *isolated skill* does not determine a
work of art. Skill is essential to a work of art, but when
it is regarded as an end in itself — that is, a technical
display — and not as a means of expression of either
meaning or function, its artistic merit might well be
questioned. "Art is the making of things well,"[2] says
Graham Carey, but he adds that the painter must be
intelligent about his own mind; that the value of his
work depends upon the fact that it is a product of the
human imagination.

The *monetary value* of a work is frequently confused with esthetic value. The cost may be due to the
antiquity or scarcity of a work and not to its artistic
merit. A comparison with the coin or stamp market
might serve as an example here. A coin may be worth

several hundred dollars not because it is a better coin, but because it is one of the few in existence.

Thorstein Veblen deals extensively with this problem in his *Theory of the Leisure Class*.[3] He shows that monetary value often overshadows both the function and the intrinsic beauty of the object.

The label or the name of the artist is a feeble measure of esthetic value, but one upon which many people depend. All the work of even a great artist is not necessarily great. A label may serve as a general guide but not as a final test. The individual must develop independent sensitivity to art qualities if understanding of art is expected.

There is no particular reason why people should be denied the right to enjoy pictures and other works for the relatively non-esthetic qualities mentioned above. But there is every reason why one should not confuse these qualities with those which the trained and sensitive observer understands as artistic qualities. The qualities mentioned above may, incidentally, exist in a work of art, but they alone are not responsible for its being so termed. Consequently, we are compelled to leave the negative side and to look for qualities that may be termed "esthetic" — qualities which may better characterize a work of art.

ESTHETIC QUALITIES

Philosophers differ in their interpretation of esthetic qualities. Two main points of view, the "genetic" and the "formal," are subject to discussion.

The genetic point of view: Santayana, who represents the genetic point of view, claims there are three kinds of beauty: (1) "Sensuous beauty of material," (2) "Formal beauty of the design," and (3) "Expressive beauty of the meaning."

Green refers to these same elements when he states that "matter," "form," and "content" are *a priori* artistic categories. Some artistic categories, he says, are more basic than others because they refer to characteristics which every work of art must, by definition, possess. "Matter," "form," and "content" are categories of this type; they are *a priori,* he says, in the sense of being necessarily and affirmatively applicable, by definition, to every work of art in any medium.

That matter, form, and content are necessary to a work of art is generally accepted by most art philosophers. The "quarrel" in esthetics is not so much concerned with the existence of these, as with their specific definition and the relationship they bear to one another. The *genetic* school represented by Dewey, Santayana, Green, and others says that matter, form, and content are inseparable and interdependent.

THE FORMAL POINT OF VIEW

The *formal* point of view, which is taken by Clive Bell and Roger Fry, differs from the genetic point of view in that *content* is not given importance. It should be remembered that Bell and Fry wrote at a time when the story telling quality was the main criterion for the judgment of painting. Their stand, therefore, seems to be a reaction against the practice of using the non-esthetic qualities mentioned above as a basis of art judgement. The Formalists claim that form alone is adequate to determine a work of art. They consider it the one common quality by which all art may be judged.

In his book, *Art,* Bell states: "For either all works of visual art have some common quality, or when we speak of 'works of art' we gibber.... There must be some one quality without which a work of art cannot exist; possessing which, in the least degree, no work is altogether worthless. What is this quality?... Only one answer seems possible — significant form. In each lines and colors combined in a particular way, certain forms and relation of forms, stir our esthetic emotions. These relations and combinations of lines and colors, these esthetically moving forms, I call 'Significant Form;' and 'Significant Form' is the one quality common to all works of visual art."[4]

What Bell terms "Significant forms" his critics term "insignificant form" because they consider he neglects content to the extent that he renders art meaningless.

Form alone is insufficient to explain art for the genetic school. Its followers agree that *form* is an important esthetic quality but, alone, they consider it inadequate.

There is a danger in interpreting form as isolated from content or meaning. This danger lies in a tendency to think of form as a kind of "streamlining," a mere manipulation of lines into pleasing patterns. Laurence Buermeyer [5] criticizes Bell for claiming that significant form may exist apart from the meaning. He says that in Bell's theory of form there is an absolute divorce between form and subject matter, to the repudiation not only of copying but of every type or degree of interpretation. "Plastic form," says Buermeyer, is only relatively independent of subject matter; and while subject matter does not in any degree furnish the detail of an artist's work, it does furnish the point of departure and, relatively, at least, fix the conditions of success. He states further, in criticism of Bell, that when the clue which subject matter offers is entirely discarded, the artist is reduced to playing with sensations, to devising patterns which may have many elements of esthetic appeal but which are far from sufficient for great art.

One might question if Bell and Fry intended to exclude content from art to the extent that their critics claim. Since, as is said above, these men wrote in an age when the general public was little concerned with other than the subject matter of a painting, "content" in art meant the presence of *objects* or *things*.

Such an idea as an "art of spiritual harmony" as created by Kandinsky, for example, might have found the early readers of Bell or Fry quite confused.

The direction a philosophy of art education takes is largely determined by the choice that is made between the ideas of the genetic and the formalist schools.

The formalists place art beyond the grasp of the "ordinary" man says Gilbert: "They admit only a few highly endowed persons as having esthetic capacity, which they define as a special sensitivity to form. The values of the world of beauty are, in their opinion, as remote from those of actual common living as the most multidimensional geometry. Such questions as: Do you like this or not? Do you find this pleasing or not? — addressed to an ordinary student would simply not touch the periphery of the esthetic realm for thinkers of this school." [6]

THE GENETIC POINT OF VIEW

The genetic school, on the other hand, thinks of art as a way of life: "The cardinal postulate with the genetic school — Dewey, Santayana, and their train of associates — from which we have drawn the critics of formalism, is that no 'value' is special or, as they say, compartmental. 'The esthetic good is hatched in the same nest with the others, and is incapable of flying far in a different air,' says Santayana." [7]

From the above statements it appears that if art
education is expected to be of value to the individual
and to society it must necessarily lean to the more
inclusive principles characteristic of the genetic school.
For practical reasons, too, such a choice seems inevitable: it would be difficult to devise a successful
method for teaching "ivory tower art" to school
children. Green's artistic categories or Santayana's
" sensuous beauty of material", "formal beauty of the
design," and "expressive beauty of meaning" provide
an excellent basis on which to build a practical philosophy of art education, for as will be seen later children
have what seems to be a natural affinity to these
esthetic qualities.

It would be well to define these three kinds of
beauty. Separation that may be implied by such defi-
nitions is a theoretical one, of course, for it has been
stated above that they are inseparable.

The first kind of beauty — *the sensuous beauty of
the material* — results from using the material or medium of art in such a way that it retains the expressiveness of its own nature. If wood, for example, is the
medium for sculpture, the finished product retains the
woodlike quality; there is conformity of the shape to
the grain of the material. Stone being the medium,
the work retains the massiveness and quality of stone.
Painters such as Van Gogh, who seem to revel in
their medium, show a strong sensitivity to this kind

of beauty: the finished product is expressive of both the brush and the paint.

Violations of this principle may frequently be seen in attempts to imitate one material with another. Metal painted to imitate wood, composition shingles made to imitate brick, clay forced to imitate metal are outstanding examples of such violations.

The second kind of beauty, *the formal beauty of the design,* is given various terms by different writers (some of them borrowed from other arts): "plastic organization," "plastic orchestration," "significant form" being the most common. The term "composition" if used broadly enough would suffice, but since composition has so frequently meant a "pleasing arrangement" of objects, it is important to be sure a fuller meaning is given. Barnes explains the meaning of the term "composition" in its wider context:

". . . composition is the whole process of ordering, organizing, and unifying the plastic elements in the form of a picture. Conventionally, the term 'composition' has been applied to the distribution of masses, but this is an unjustifiable limitation of its meaning. The compositional units of a picture may, but need not, be masses; they may also be areas of color, islands of light, linear arabesques, or any means whatever by which balance and unity are secured."[8]

In a discussion of composition the distinction between arrangement and organization is of utmost importance. An arrangement may result from the juxtaposition of objects and as such not have the *formal beauty of the design*. Not mere adjacency of objects but articulation of line, form, color, and light is necessary. Adjustment, selection, or anatomical distortion of the parts is necessary to procure formal relationship.

This distortion or adjustment is not peculiar to the visual arts. A writer of fiction finds distortion and adjustment quite as necessary as does the painter. It would be difficult to have structure or unity (form) in a novel without the imagination of the author to create situations that may have been inspired by fact. Facts in isolation have little meaning, but when their relationships are expressed — that is, when they are given form — they become of value.

In like manner the sounds of nature must be changed and new ones created to form a unified musical composition. Whether the "raw" materials of an art be paint, words, or sounds, *design* is necessary to transfigure mere mechanical arrangement and documentation.

The third kind of beauty, *the expressive beauty of the idea or meaning,* relates art to the deeper and more intense qualities of human experience.

Expressive beauty of the meaning does not mean simply the presence of certain objects recognizable as such. Because a picture tells a story, for example, it is not necessarily *expressive* of the meaning. Expres-

sive beauty, says Edman, is a result of the treatment
of the subject matter rather than the existence of it. [9]

The absence of recognizable objects in a painting
does not necessarily imply that expressive meaning is
lacking. Abstract or non-objective painting may have
the expressive beauty of meaning. It all depends on
what meaning is intended to be expressed. Perhaps
the artist did not intend to express the external ap-
pearance of an object or person but rather the internal or psychological characteristics. An artist may
wish to express his understanding of the order in the
universe. To do so would require that the picture be
composed not of recognizable objects but, instead, of
movements and forces of line, form, color, and light.

Young children do not hesitate to paint non-objective ideas and movements rather than things. "I
painted how I love my mother," said the four-year-
old, showing her non-objective painting to her teacher.
Certainly such a painting is not devoid of meaning.

Louis Danz distinguishes betweeen the painting of
an object (or "noun") and the painting of a movement (or "verb") and points out that the latter may
also have meaning in a painting.

"One day an Imaginative-one (verb painter) came
upon a group of Imagination-ones (noun painters)
who were painting.

'What are you doing?' asked the Imaginative one.
'We are learning to paint.'

'What are you painting?'

'I am painting a picture of that house,' said one.

'I am doing that tree,' said another.

'I am painting that dog playing in the grass,' said a third.

Then the Imaginative-one asked, 'Will you paint some for me?'

'We will paint anything for you,' was the response.

But the Imaginative-one, shaking his head, said 'I did not ask you to paint any *thing*. I did not even ask you to paint some *thing*. I merely asked if you would paint *some* for me.'

'But if we are not to paint anything...'

'Nor something...'

'What can we paint?' were the puzzled questions.

Then he answered, 'Paint for me a solid or a volume, a weight, a direction, a tempo. Paint for me cohesion, adhesion, attraction, antipathy, elasticity, gravity, rhythm...' " [10]

It is doubtful if either one in isolation has meaning in any complete sense. One might agree with Louis Danz that the uninterpreted snapshot view of an object does not express meaning. The moment the more "intense seeing" takes place, the object as a thing (noun) is combined with movement (verb) so that expressive meaning may be said to be a noun-verb combination.

It is important in art to understand expressive

meaning in this broader sense; otherwise some of the greater spiritual values that art has to offer may be lost. To understand expressive meaning, *one must develop a "seeing" that is more than a simple recognition of objects,* a vision that grasps meaning in "movement," form relationships, and color. Roger Fry points out in *Vision and Design* that in the ordinary seeing we do during the day we do not in any esthetic sense use our eyes at all. We see as much of objects as we need to get around. What there is in the way of color and line and shape and volume we do not see at all. [11]

EMPATHY

The development of *einfuehlung* or empathy may serve as a step toward a more adequate seeing as well as help one grasp the "expressive beauty of meaning" in the visual arts. Empathy is defined as "feeling oneself into," or having a kinesthetic response to an object. Danz terms it "movement inside one's skin."[12]

An example of such "movement inside one's skin" may be illustrated by the feeling one might have while watching a gull soaring through the air. According to the theory of empathy, the observer experiences the movement, balance, and poise of the soaring bird and derives pleasure from such movement and balance.

A person with a developed power of empathy might have a vicarious ride on a roller coaster, "experiencing" many of the dips and thrills while standing on the side line observing the movements of the cars on the curving track.

Appreciation of the "flight" quality in such creations as Brancusi's "Bird in Space" requires a similar empathic or kinesthetic reaction. One who has not learned to react to form empathically would have difficulty understanding and enjoying "Bird in Space."

An empathic or kinesthetic response alone does not insure *esthetic enjoyment.* If the object is not graceful or balanced or unified, if it does not have "form," a feeling of displeasure is quite likely to be experienced.

Allport mentions both pleasant and unpleasant empathy. "Contemplation of a work of art involves innumerable slight movements of brows, the eyes, the trunk and limbs, as well as internal changes which elude observation. Graceful, uninterrupted, but not too simple, empathic movements are said to give rise to judgements of pleasantness and beauty; movements that are jerky, asymmetrical, or over-simple make the object seem disagreeable or ugly." [13]

There are opposing opinions as to whether *empathic* seeing differs in kind or in degree from *ordinary* seeing. Santayana claims the difference is one of degree rather than one of kind and that all images to some degree are motor. In any case we can agree that all normal individuals have the potentiality for reacting empathically or kinesthetically to the world about them.

It is not important to decide whether empathy is a different kind of seeing or a more intense variety of an ordinary kind. It is important, however, that empathic or kinesthetic powers be developed, for art understanding and creativity depend to a large degree upon such powers.

More than an empathic response is necessary for the creation or the appreciation of art, since as is said above, this response may lead to an unpleasant reaction as well as a pleasant or esthetic one.

Esthetic creation or contemplation requires not only empathic seeing but also ability to grasp and unify formal and meaningful relationships. Empathy alone is not sufficient to insure a unity in what is created or observed and, if we agree with the genetic point of view, such a unity is necessary. The ability to grasp the unified whole empathically depends upon developed powers of *intuition*.

INTUITION

A distinction between the popular and the philosophical definition of intuition should be clearly understood.

Popularly *intuition* means "a woman's hunch" or an idea entirely unsupported by fact. Dependence upon intuition so understood often leads to "wild" guesses or unfounded suspicions. A grasp of art values certainly cannot result from such willy-nilly judgments.

Herbert Read defines intuition, as it pertains to art, not as any super-sensational faculty of the mind, but as the apprehension of abstract quantities and relations (size, shape, distance, volume, surface-area, etc.)

Every normal individual uses intuition in making the judgments that are necessary in his everyday activity. In our daily routine, however, we are likely to be unaware that we are constantly depending upon intuition. But in moments of intensity or crisis when there seems to be no other course and we bring together all experiences of the past and possibilities of the present into an instantaneous and necessary action, we readily recognize this unifying power as *intuition*. Whether such an action be driving an automobile through a precarious situation, sending a ball down a bowling alley to a strike, successfully handling a difficult social problem, or bringing visual elements together on a canvas, all require intuition.

Intuition is not a product of instant revelation having no roots or foundation. Rather it is the product of a long incubation, of observation and imagination. Dewey states that the artist derives his substance from a long stream of culture. He is dependent upon tradition just as the scientific inquirer, the philosopher, and the technologist depend upon tradition. Such dependence, he says, is an essential factor in original vision and creative expression.

" 'Intuition' is that meeting of old and new in which the readjustment involved in every form of consciousness is effected suddenly by means of a quick and unexpected harmony which in its bright abruptness is like a flash of revelation; although in fact it is prepared for by long and slow incubation. Oftentimes the union of old and new, of foreground and background, is accomplished only by effort, prolonged perhaps to the point of pain. In any case, the background of organized meanings can alone convert the new situation from the obscure into the clear and luminous. When the old and new jump together, like sparks when poles are adjusted, there is intuition." [14]

In teaching art it is important to recognize that the ability to intuit is not limited to the few; that all in some degree at least are "artists," for it is a quality of human nature to make, to form, and to express.

"Nor can we admit that the word genius or artistic genius, as distinct from the non-genius of the ordinary man, possesses more than a quantitative signification. Great artists are said to reveal us to ourselves. But how could this be possible, unless there were identity of nature between their imagination and ours, and unless the difference were only one of quantity? It were better to change *poeta nascitur* into *homo nascitur poeta:* some men are born great poets, some small. The cult of the genius with all of its attendant superstitions has arisen from this quantitative difference having been taken as a difference in quality. It has been forgotten that genius is not something fallen from heaven, but humanity itself." [15]

The fact that communication between individuals by the use of visual means is possible at all, that "there is identity between their nature and ours," indicates the necessary existence of some underlying basis for judgment of works of art. This basis is intangible and cannot be measured quantitatively, and yet it exists as surely as works of art have been selected and treasured throughout the centuries. Such a basis seems to consist of an inner assurance of the rightness of things; a feeling for the unity of matter, form, and content, or in other words, *intuition*. Without it there would be no essential difference between a Giotto fresco and the picture on the average roadside sign.

"Without intelligence, imagination runs wild; without imagination, intelligence is sterile; and without intuition — which is the rarest and most sublime mental quality — both intelligence and imagination are denied the discovery of the hidden behind the already revealed verities. Intuition in the most exact sense is 'genius,' 'grace,' or charisma. It creates; whereas intelligence proper and imagination understand, relate, combine, and interpret." [16]

SUMMARY

Meaningful art education distinguishes between

non-esthetic qualities and *esthetic* qualities. It does not deny the individual the right to enjoy the former, but it attempts to guide the individual to the understanding and enjoyment of essentially *esthetic* qualities, namely, *beauty of material, beauty of form,* and *beauty of meaning,* and the unity of these. The understanding of these requires the development of empathic, or *more adequate seeing,* and *intuition.*

REFERENCE BOOKS, CHAPTER II

[1]Dewey, John, *Art as Experience.* New York: G. P. Putnam's Sons, 1935. p. 103.

[2]Carey, Graham, *The Majority Report on Art.* Newport, Rhode Island: John Stephens, 1937.

[3]Veblen, Thorstein, *The Theory of the Leisure Class:* An Economic Study of Institutions. New York: The Modern Library, 1934.

[4]Bell, Clive, *Art.* London: Chatto and Windus, 1920. pp. 8-9.

[5]Buermeyer, Laurence, *Art and Education.* Merion, Pa.: The Barnes Foundation Press, 1929.

[6]Gilbert, Katherine, *Studies in Recent Aesthetics.* Chapel Hill, N. C.: The University of North Carolina Press, 1927. p. 17.

[7]*Ibid.,* pp. 25-26.

[8]Barnes, Albert, *The Art in Painting.* New York: Harcourt, Brace and Co., 1937. p. 72.

[9]Edman, Erwin, *Arts and the Man.* New York: W. W. Norton and Co., 1939.

[10]Danz, Louis, *The Psychologist Looks at Art.* New York: Longmans, Green, and Co., 1937. pp. 43-44.

[11]Fry, Roger, *Vision and Design.* New York: Coward-McCann, Inc., 1924.

[12]*Op. cit.,* Danz, Louis. p. 115.

[13]Allport, Gordon W., *Personality*. New York: Henry Holt and Co., 1937. p. 531.

[14]*Op. cit.*, Dewey, John. p. 266.

[15]Croce, Benedetto, *Aesthetic*. London: Macmillan and Co. Limited, 1922. p. 8.

[16]Ulich, Robert, *Conditions of Civilized Living*. New York: E. P. Dutton and Co., Inc., 1946. pp. 68-69.

CHAPTER III

The Value of
Meaningful Art Education
for the Individual

ART IS increasingly recognized as important for personal growth. When there is concern with unity of matter, form, and content (as was discussed in Chapter II) art seems to have exceptional possibilities for the formation of personality. It may lead to the development of characteristics which Allport [1] says are essential to maturity, namely, autonomous interests, self-objectification, and a unifying philosophy of life.

The emphasis in this chapter is with the latter of these characteristics, for if the individual has a unifying philosophy of life, it may be presupposed that he also has autonomous interests and the power of self-objectification or insight. By its very nature art provides autonomous interests for the individual. Interest in art and "extension of the self" may be considered synonymous. The artist, be he adult or child, may lose himself in his thought and in his work. Art also may contribute to the development of the power of self-objectification or insight in the individual. The artist who works sincerely may see himself reflected in his own creations.

Art as it contributes to the development of a unifying philosophy of life (as was stated above) is the main concern of this chapter. It has three outstanding advantages for personality integration which will be discussed.

First, *it can be a unifying process.* It is concerned with the selection and organization of material, form, and content. Secondly, *it has the advantage of tangibility or concrete objectification.* The art product provides the individual with a reassurance of the existence of the unity he has discovered as well as with a means of communicating the idea of the unity to others. Thirdly, *art can be a pervasive element in the life of the individual.* [2]

Before discussing these three advantages of art for individual integration, it may be well to digress for a moment to consider on what level, in the growth of the individual, integration is expected to take place.

Allport [3] describes, in the order of their complexity, several levels in the growth of an individual where integration may take place. These levels range through

simple conditioned reflexes, habits, traits, selves, and
personality. He states that the simplest possible integration may be represented by two nerve cells func-
tioning together as a simple reflex arc. At the opposite extreme, integration may be represented by a
completely unified personality. Either of these extremes,
he says, are convenient though improbable abstrac-
tions, but somewhere between them there is ample
room for actual integration.

It would be difficult to determine what effect art
might have upon each of these different levels of
growth, especially upon those in the "lower" end of
the scale beginning with conditioned reflexes.

Art concerned with the unity of matter, form, and
content (rather than art as a practice) probably has
its integrating effect upon areas of the personality
that are more the concern of philosophy and religion
than of experimental psychology in its present stage
of development. This would place the integrating
influence of art, perhaps, on a level above that of
exact and experimental psychology.

Allport recognizes the possibilities of integration
on a metaphysical level. He states that while this
level is not within the scope of experimental psychology it should not be ignored but dealt with as a separate factor. He says that there are many meanings
of the term *personality* other than the special psychological meaning.

"Metaphysically one might define personality as 'the indestructable essence of individual being (the soul).' Such a definition would of necessity claim unity as an essential attribute of personality. This proposition, though it may very well be true, lies altogether in a non-psychological realm of discourse. In deciding to dispense with the soul, psychologists cut themselves off deliberately from such speculative propositions of theology and philosophy. Unfortunately they fall at the same time into the rather shabby habit of declaring that all the metaphysical conceptions with which they refused to deal were *ipso facto* meaningless. It would be far wiser to concede that metaphysical unity may be a property of personality, while insisting that it is a different problem from the empirical unity that falls within the province of psychology." [4]

Assuming the possibility of integration on this higher level, it is well now to return to the three advantages mentioned above that art may have for personality development.

ART IS A UNIFYING PROCESS

Art is concerned not only with the plastic unity of the object itself but, as well, with the formal relationship and the content relationship of the object to the individual and to his environment.

In art creativity, the individual must select or reject, respectively, what may contribute or detract

from the unity of his creation. Such selection may not
be possible in the individual's ordinary work and associations; here he may meet with disintegrating influences and events over which he has little control.
At every turn he may find his efforts unfulfilled and
seemingly futile. To preserve his courage, somewhere,
the individual must find meaning, order, and unity.
Art may provide the assurance that order and unity
do exist for those who would find them. This does not
mean that art is recommended as an escape from life;
rather it implies, as Dewey[5] suggests, that art may be a
means by which the individual may turn the powers of
nature into account and thereby construct a fortress
out of the very conditions and forces which threaten
him.

The art creator seeks good where otherwise there
might be evil; he finds order where otherwise there
might be chaos. His aim is opposite the aim of Milton's satan in *Paradise Lost*:

> If then his providence
> Out of our evil seek to bring forth good,
> Our labor must be to pervert that end,
> And out of good still find a means of evil.

The importance of a deliberate seeking for order,
even out of chaos, is essential for man, says Dewey;[6]
in his invention of the arts he has discovered a way
of finding and objectifying such order. In a world
constantly threatened with disorder, living creatures

can go on living only by taking advantage of whatever order exists about them, incorporating it into themselves, he says.

Hopkins,[7] like Allport and Dewey, recognizes the integrating value of art for the individual. He states that this value depends upon a comprehensive idea of unity and that the vision of the possibility of such unity is a factor strongly motivating to art creativity. He also emphasizes the importance of the creative process as well as the resulting product. "Wholeness," he says, "permeates the activity, the experience, and the product when full creativeness is carried on."

Dewey speaks of the importance of art as *an* experience, as an integrating value for the individual. He differentiates between "*an* experience," as a total pattern of material experience running its course to fulfillment, and mere happenings or what is ordinarily termed experience. To have *an* experience is to approximate a complete unity. The motivation, the doing, the product, and the purpose complement one another. We have *an* experience, he says, when the material experienced runs its course to fulfillment.

"An experience has a unity that gives it its name ....The existence of this unity is constituted by a single quality that pervades the entire experience in spite of the variation of its constituent parts." [8]

Raup's[9] theory of complacency has a similarity to Dewey's definition of an experience. He claims that life to be meaningful is necessarily made up of a succession of patterns comprised of *disturbance, relief from disturbance,* and *return to complacency.* In such a pattern it is evident that a "disturbance" is not enjoyed for its own sake; neither is there particular satisfaction in the state of complacency. (This state is short-lived in any case.) Rather, according to Raup's theory, satisfaction is found in relieving the disturbance — in finding a balance or a unity. This is an important point, for too often the product is set apart from the process; the state of complacency apart from the satisfying period of finding unity.

The theory of *an* experience translated into practical terms for the classroom seems to show the necessity of providing the child with the possibility of art creativity that is meaningful to him. It places emphasis upon the art process as well as upon the art product and upon the relationship of process and product.

If the child is to have *an* experience there must be some relationship between the child's interests, his means of carrying them out, and, in turn, the finished product. For the child to create "meaningfully" he must have something to say; he must know how to use the tools and materials of artistic expression (comparable to his age level and aptitude), and he must have some idea of what might be expected in the finished product.

Blind procedures in regard to idea, materials,

and product do not make for the totality of *an* experience, and art so pursued is not a unifying process.

A child who sets out to make a toy boat because he lives near the water and wants a boat is likely to have *an* experience in the whole procedure. His purpose provides him with inventiveness, and the vision of the finished product the incentive for carrying it out. If he is fortunate enough to have the guidance of some adult who knows about materials, tools, boats — and children, his *experience* may be enriched. He may be guided to make a better boat, and his satisfaction both in the doing and in the product is greater. He has "an experience."

This same principle applies when he paints a picture. The content of the picture must be his own idea. To be sure, the teacher may have inspired it, but *inspired* it must be. To expect a child to express something that not he, but someone else, thinks or feels is a first violation of art as a unifying process.

The motivating idea and the finished product are closely related and unity of each is reflected in the other. "A vision of the possibility of wholeness is the prod to upset in the case of the artist or the creating child," says Hopkins.

"Neither reacts to the environment in the raw nor merely to a large and varied mass of material, but each is stirred by finding in a fragmentary and transitory setting certain elements in a situation that 'make sense' through their connectedness. An underlying pattern is from that moment projected imaginatively, and the totality of the creative experience itself is incomplete until the wholeness sensed in the situation is objectified."[10]

In painting a picture as in making a toy boat, the motivating idea and the vision of a finished product provide a need in the child for knowledge of ways and means of handling materials and tools to carry out the task. In this respect even "techniques" become a part of a unifying process. When guidance in "techniques" falls short of the child's need and his capacity for doing, or when it proceeds too far beyond his need and capacity, the unifying element is violated and the child does not have *an* experience.

Because art as a unifying process admits the necessity of selection and organization, it does not follow, as was mentioned above, that it is to be used as an escape from life.

"Ivory tower" art denies the value of art as *an* experience in that it places value exclusively on the product. It attempts to find a smug little world in the art object. The objection to art's being used as an escape from life does not intend that the individual be prevented from making a selection of what seems to him to be values. Rather it implies that such selection be made from the more inclusive areas that make up the whole.

The artist who isolates himself from the world is not likely to find art a factor in personality development. Whatever unity exists within his canvas exists apart from the greater unity which makes art *an* experience. An art product conceived as separate from the intention of the creating individual is like subject matter learned without understanding. Both may possess unity within their own limits but they cannot be of integrative value for the individual because they are apart from the individual.

The artist has control over the elements that go into his creation. To repeat a statement made earlier in the chapter, the artist may select from his environment that which contributes to the unified whole. This advantage that the artist has may defeat his own purposes unless "whole" is interpreted in a broad sense. The artist who is concerned only with the unity in the *product* rejects elements that are necessary to the greater unity. He isolates himself rather than unites himself and his work with his environment.

Santayana[11] distinguishes between a unity which is brought about by exclusion of all the non-unifying elements and one that is brought about by including the given elements. He says that there are always two methods of securing harmony: one is to unify the given elements and the other is to reject all the elements that refuse to be unified. Unity by inclusion, he says, gives us the beautiful; unity by exclusion and isolation gives us the sublime; the former identifies us with the world, the latter raises us above it.

It is self-evident that art education that is concerned with individual and social integration must choose unity by *inclusion*. Edman says that the esthete who attempts to find unity by "exclusion" meets with questionable success, and that the theory of art as escape fails to take into account much that is true of esthetic experience. He says, "It abstracts the aesthetic man much as the early nineteenth century abstracted economic man." He states that no one is ever for long an esthetic observer, and that part of esthetic enjoyment is the rendition of the world we know and the nature we are.

The eye of the beholder is the eye of a human being, with all the vast reverberation of human interests and emotions. The ear of the listener is the ear of one to whom sounds have associations and of one who has listened to words for their meanings as well as for their tintinnabulations."[12]

There is a parallel to "ivory tower" art in "ivory tower" learning. The one places emphasis upon the unity in the art product and the other places emphasis upon the unity in the subject matter. Burton deals with this problem in reference to the guidance of learning. He states that the factor determining unity in a teaching-learning situation must lie in either of two sources — in the subject matter or in the learner.

"Unity in subject matter lies in the logical arrangement of the materials around a center or core which resides within the subject matter itself. . . .

"Unity in the learner lies in the primary integration within himself and between him and his environment."[13]

If art creativity, like learning, is to contribute to the integration of personality, unity in the art product alone, like unity of subject matter alone, is inadequate to the task.

The integrative value of meaningful and effortful activity may be further substantiated by what Ulich says about the importance of *work*. The same principle may be applied to art creativity, which may be considered a form of work with a maximum of satisfying possibilities. He states that work is not only a means of earning a livelihood but that it has consequences far beyond those of a merely physical nature; that it provides the necessary exercise for mind and muscles and saves the individual from the torture of uselessness, aloneness, and boredom. It gives the individual, he continues, the opportunity for integrating his various and often diverging urges and desires through the provision of a permanent task and purpose.

Too often, "art" like "work" is considered only for its dollar and cents value, and while this aspect may not be entirely ignored it must not overshadow the fact that subsistence alone is not man's final aim.

Although it might be said that any form of work is better than complete idleness, there are various degrees in which different kinds of work may give satisfaction and in turn be of integrating value for the individual. The man on the assembly line, for example, for the most part, must view his accomplishment in terms of an accumulation of tasks done. More frequently than not even this view is an abstract one of figures on a paper showing the number of operations he has made throughout the day, for the products of his efforts disappear to the shipping room. Unfortunately, it is not possible in a modern industrial age to give every worker a complete picture of his daily accomplishment; if it were, it is likely that many problems of personal adjustment might be solved.

It is in this connection that art creativity has the advantage over other kinds of work. Here is a field where the "worker" may always view his handiwork as a whole. The motivation, the doing, the product, and the purpose may form an experience and as such be a value for the individual.

TANGIBILITY IS AN ADVANTAGE OF VISUAL ART

The second advantage that visual art may have for individual integration is its tangibility or concreteness. The art object serves to keep intact a cue to the esthetic experience which originally inspired its creation. One may turn to the tangible art object and instantly grasp the unified idea that is here expressed.

The space arts — painting, sculpture, and architecture — unlike the time arts — music, literature, and the dance — are ever ready for immediate and relatively complete contemplation. In contrast to the time arts, the space arts supply what seems to be a vital human need of a tangible evidence of otherwise fleeting meanings and values. Music must be reinterpreted, a book reread, the dance reperformed, but the space art object exists always in its original and tangible form. This does not imply that the space arts are in any way superior to the time arts. No such comparison can be made, for both are important. Man is not so sophisticated that he can live without symbols, and he needs the variety of symbols that all of the arts provide. It does say, however, that the space arts have the unique advantage of "tangibility."

Dependence upon symbols, and particularly upon those symbols which take on physical form, is deeply rooted in human nature, says Coomaraswamy.

"...realism is inseparable from human nature, and it would be easy to show that this is always and everywhere the case. The mere existence of science does not defend us from it: the majority will always conceive of atoms and electrons as real things, which would be tangible if they were not so small, and will always believe that tangibility is a proof of existence; and are fully convinced that a being, originating at a given moment of time, may yet, as that same being, survive eternally in time. He who believes that phenomena of necessity stand for solid existing actualities, or that there can exist any empirical consciousness or individuality without a material (substantial) basis, or that anything that has come into being can endure as such forever, is an idolater, a fetishist."[14]

"It may be said that images are to the Hindu what diagrams are to the geometrician."[15]

The art product considered as a symbol admits the necessity of *association* in art. This takes us back to a problem that was discussed in Chapter II, p. 19, that there is a difference between using the art object as a simple reminder of some other simple event and as a reference to more cosmic content.

Attempt to decide whether such a difference is one of kind or of degree will not be made here. It would seem, however, that sentimental association as was mentioned on page 19 finds the art product and the object to which it refers parallel to one another or on the same level. Esthetic association, on the other hand, finds the art object as a cue to ever-expanding universal values. To clarify further, non-esthetically a painting of a tree reminds the observer of another tree; esthetically a painting of a tree lifts the individual object out of its isolation into the persuasive texture of universal ideas. Esthetic association shows a relation of the art product to something greater than itself, something that transcends the limits of material form. The unifying value to the individual of the art object as an objectification of the unity discovered seems to depend upon this more expansive association.

Edman mentions the value of the art object as a reference to wider associations. He says that the very rationality which the philosopher seeks to find or make possible in the universe the artist in his area and within the scope of his materials is trying to achieve.

"The organization of each little created world is a *simulacrum,* a cameo version of the order which philosophers have tried with pathetic insistence, to find or read into the universe."[16]

The art object, therefore, is of value to the individual to the extent that it serves as a tangible reference to a greater unity. In such a role it cannot be separated from the first advantage mentioned here — that art may be a unifying process.

ART IS A PERVASIVE ELEMENT

The third advantage that art may have for personality integration is that *it may be a pervasive element in the life of the individual.* Art is such, probably, because it may be a unifying process and because it may objectify in plastic materials the unity it finds. In this way the three advantages that art may have for integrating the personality are inseparable and interdependent.

Ulich recognizes both the external and internal aspects of art as a pervasive element, together with its influence on personality. He says that everything is, in one way or another, touched by art. "At present, art in some fashion surrounds us more than religion and perhaps even more than reason." He adds that this visible influence of art on our external life is but part of the story; there is something more penetrating about it, namely its subtle effect on the mold of personality.

Santayana,[17] too, sees art as inseparable from other life interests not to be compared externally but "woven into the texture of everything." Like Ulich, he considers art important as influence on the personality. He says that esthetic sensibility colors every thought, qualifies every allegiance, and modifies every product of human labor.

If art is a pervasive element as these philosophers state, its influence on human personality is inevitable. For this reason its unifying characteristics must be fully realized and utilized in art education.

SUMMARY

The emphasis here upon the unity of matter, form, and content, the relation of process and product, means and end, the value of art as *an* experience is made in the hope that through art the individual may formulate a unifying philosophy of life, and the implications of this fact must be fully utilized in the education of youth.

REFERENCE BOOKS, CHAPTER III

[1]Allport, Gordon W., *Personality:* A Psychological Interpretation. New York: Henry Holt and Co., 1937. pp. 139-140.

[2]Ulich, Robert, *Conditions of Civilized Living.* New York: E. P. Dutton and Co., Inc., 1946.

[3]*Op. cit.,* Allport, Gordon W. pp. 139-140.

[4]*Ibid.* p. 348.

[5]Dewey, John, *Art As Experience.* New York: G. P. Putnam's Sons, 1934.

[6]*Ibid.*

[7]Hopkins, L. Thomas, *Integration.* New York: D. Appleton-Century Co., 1937. pp. 148-152.

[8]*Op. cit.,* Dewey, John. pp. 35-37.

[9]Raup, Robert, *Complacency.* New York: The Macmillan Co., 1925.

[10]*Op. cit.,* Hopkins, L. Thomas. pp. 148-152.

[11]Santayana, George, *The Sense of Beauty.* New York: Charles Scribner's Sons, 1896. pp. 235-236.

[12]Edman, Erwin, *Arts and the Man.* New York: W. W. Norton and Co., Inc., 1939. pp. 24-25.

[13]Burton, William H., *The Guidance of Learning Activities.* D. Appleton-Century Co., 1944. pp. 244-245.

[14]Coomaraswamy, Ananda, *The Transformation of Nature in Art.* Cambridge, Mass.: Harvard University Press, 1934. p. 156.

[15]*Ibid.* p. 155. Rao, Elements of Hindu Iconography.

[16]*Op cit.,* Edman, Erwin. pp. 121-122.

[17]Santayana, George, *The Life of Reason,* New York: Charles Scribner's Sons, 1926.

CHAPTER IV

The Value of a Meaningful
Art Education for Society

IN A WORLD of social change such as we have to-day, it is sometimes difficult for the teacher to see what contribution his efforts may make to the betterment of society. Whatever this contribution, it may seem like such a small "drop in the bucket" as hardly to be worth while at all. Daily he sees the children he has taught go into a world unfriendly to the principles that in the classroom seemed so important for living together.

Teachers may face this problem in many different ways. Some are like the spider building a web; when it is torn down they struggle along and build it up again — in the same place. Others bitterly complain of a mysterious "they," as if the powers of evil in the world were aligned into one faction bent on destroying any good the individual might do. At best, human progress is slow, but education can justify its existence only by attempting to make some contribution, however small, to that progress.

Art education is no exception; blind procedure or an attitude of futility in reference to human and social values, in this field as in any other field of education, is hardly justifiable. On the other hand, overambitious hopes (as are sometimes expressed) that art will create "one world" are quite likely to lead to discouragement. With certain limitations well in mind, then, attempt is made here to suggest some value a meaningful art education may have for society.

Just as a meaningful art education has advantages for individual integration, it has advantages for social integration. For society, as well as an individual, needs a unifying philosophy of life which art, considered in its unifying characteristics, is able to provide.

In addition, just as individual integration due to art seems to take place on an "upper psychological or metaphysical" level of the personality (to use Allport's terms), so social integration due to art seems to take place on an upper level of the "culture mentality."

The problem, then, is to point out (1) that there is a relationship between art and society, (2) that higher social integration depends upon a reemphasis of inner values — values that cannot be measured quantitatively, and (3) that meaningful art education is concerned with such values.

ART REFLECTS THE SOCIETY

That there is a relationship between art and society can hardly be doubted. Sorokin states that the fine arts are one of the most sensitive mirrors of the society and culture of which they are an important part. "What the society and the culture are, such will their fine arts be..... If the culture is unintegrated, chaotic, and eclectic, also will be its fine arts."[1] Art is not only a mirror reflecting society as it *is*, but it is also a mirror into which society may look to correct its ills. To say otherwise is to deny the possibility of education. For education must depend upon the orderly objectification of its ideas to give direction to its practices.

INTEGRATION IN ART AND SOCIETY

Accepting the thesis that there is a mutual dependence of integration in society and integration in art, the formulation of a theory of art education having social value hinges upon certain characteristics or needs of a society. In this connection it is of first importance to ask what characteristics a society lacks when it is unintegrated. Attempt to answer this question has been made by many philosophers, and the opinions of a few of them will be given here.

But first it might be well to clarify what is meant by a "higher type of integration." An analysis made by Sorokin of four basic types of interrelation of culture elements seems to fulfill this purpose. These types he enumerates as "Spatial or Mechanical Adjacency," "Association Due to an External Factor," "Causal or Functional Integration," and "Internal or Logico-meaningful Unity."

He gives us an example of Spatial or Mechanical Adjacency, "a dump in which are fragments of a great variety of objects — pieces of paper, broken bottles, empty cans, fragments of clothing, discarded spoons, wire, garbage, furniture, ashes, coal, tools. . . . All these objects just drifted or were thrown together, and this is the only bond that unites them."

For the second type, Association Due to an External Factor, he mentions by way of explanation, "vodka as a beverage, skiis used by the peasants in the wintertime, houses built out of heavy timber, large stoves for heating, felt winter boots. . ." These, he says, are not related to each other logically or functionally but rather by an external factor — the cold weather in northern Russia.

In explanation of a third and higher type of inter-relation, Causal or Functional Integration, he describes the parts of a finished automobile assembled into one whole. If these parts were lying separated on the floor, they would not be causally or functionally integrated, but spatially adjacent. It is when they are assembled for some purpose or function that they are causally integrated.

The fourth and highest type he terms Logico-meaningful Unity. He states that this type of inter-relation frequently is not recognized by people who deal with the subject of integration, but that it is most important to the understanding of the fine arts, and to social integration.

"This is integration in its supreme form. In what does it consist? What are its qualities? Suppose we have before us the scattered pages of a great poem, or of Kant's *Critique of Pure Reason,* or fragments of the statue of Venus of Milo, or the scattered pages of the score of Beethoven's *Third Symphony.* If we know the proper patterns of meaning and value, we can put these pages or parts together into a significant unity in which each page or fragment takes its proper place, acquires a meaning, and in which all together give the supremely integrated effect that was intended. I say 'supremely integrated' because in such instances each part, when set in its designated position, is no longer noticeable as a part, but all the parts together form as it were a seamless garment."[2]

He states that the two higher types of integration, namely the causal-functional and the logico-meaning-ful types, both act as the "means of ordering into comprehensible systems the infinitely numerous and complex phenomena of the sociocultural world." He adds that if we did not have such a means of ordering these diverse forms and elements we should long ago have been lost in chaos. He sees an increasing lack of such values in a "dying sensate culture." He views the present crisis not merely as an economic or political maladjustment but as one that involves simultaneously almost the whole of Western culture.

"It is a crisis in their art and science, philosophy and religion, law and morals, manners and mores; in the forms of social, political, and economic organization, including the nature of the family and marriage — in brief it is a crisis involving almost the whole way of life, thought, and conduct of Western society."[3]

The present crisis, Sorokin holds, is due to an "overripe" *sensate* culture — a culture in which values that make for a higher type of integration are lost. He describes the sensate mentality as one which views reality as only that which is presented to the sense organs, one that does not seek to believe in any supersensory reality. As a way out of social crisis he suggests a re-examination of the pseudo values of a sensate culture and the re-establishment of values that make for a higher type of integration — values that are inherent in "ideational" or "idealistic" culture.*

_____

*Sorokin describes ideational culture as non-sensate nonmaterial with needs and ends mainly spiritual. See page 73 in *Social and Cultural Dynamics,* Vol. I. Idealistic culture is de-

While other philosophers concerned with the present social crisis may not subscribe wholly to the above theory that the present crisis is due to a general disintegration of an "overripe" sensate culture, there is a fairly general agreement in the recent writings of others that there is a need for a recognition of values other than sensate ones. Some of these philosophers subscribe to a belief in transcendental values and, therefore, like Sorokin, take the idealistic standpoint. Others, who are relativistic in their thinking and who would probably deny ideational values, nevertheless admit values not verifiable by sense.

IDEALISTIC AND HUMANISTIC POINTS OF VIEW

Ulich, in the following statement, takes an idealistic stand. He, too, states the need of values which are not necessarily verifiable by sense.

"We are so narrow and one-sided because after learning how to master nature we have neglected to learn how to master ourselves and to see where the roots of our total existence are. Thus the period of technology has become a period of superficiality, ending in the greatest destruction of goods which mankind ever wrought upon itself.

"Hence, together with the progress of engineering

---

scribed as "a more or less balanced unification of Ideational and Sensate, with, however, a predominance of the Ideational elements." See page 75 in *Social and Cultural Dynamics,* Vol. I.

and industrialization, which may bring better housing and food for more and more people, we have to acquire a more profound and comprehensive image of man. For this we need the wisdom and depth which is in the awareness of the transcendent forces of life just as much as we need a rational and empirical attitude."[4]

John Dewey leans more toward Humanism and its inherent relativism than do either Ulich or Sorokin. He, probably, would not use the term "transcendent forces of life" or subscribe to Sorokin's term "supersensory reality." But he, too, in his humanistic point of view, expresses concern lest "sensate" values outstrip less tangible ones. He states that "physical knowledge and physical technology have far outstripped social or human knowledge and human engineering."[5]

Lewis Mumford,[6] like Dewey, supports the humanistic side, but he, also, emphasizes the need of other than sensate values. He says that the inner crisis of our civilization must be resolved before the outer crisis can be met effectively, and that it is our first duty to revamp our ideas and values and to reorganize the human personality around its highest needs.

The difference between the humanistic point of view of Dewey and Mumford, and the idealistic point of view of Ulich and Sorokin is not of too much concern to our purposes here. For Ulich and Sorokin do not think of transcendental values as revealed from without but rather as something that results from an ever widening experience that develops into increasingly larger and comprehensive meanings.

On the other hand, as long as Dewey's "means and end" remain intact, there need be little concern for the outcome, except that without an advance concept of values, such as may be offered by Ulich or Sorokin, there is always a danger of extreme relativism and consequent disintegration. To lean too strongly to a humanistic side, then, may lead to a relativism that may, if allowed to go unchecked, lead to disintegration. In an idealistic stand, by contrast, there is sometimes a danger of codifying "ideals" to the extent of turning them into "absolutes," with a consequent loss of inner values and their higher integrating capacity.

Only broad purpose well rooted in the thinking and action of individuals and society can effect the subtle balance necessary to keep the importance of inner values in the foreground. In turn, only the realization of inner values may lead to broad purpose. Quite as important as realizing the need of inner values for integrating society is to find practical ways of transmitting a sense of such values to successive generations.

DEVELOPMENT OF SOCIAL VALUES IN ART EDUCATION

Too often the importance of developing better social attitudes in children is underestimated. Spectacular projects for social reform on an international basis, however essential, should in no way minimize the importance of individual effort in the classroom. If art is a mirror of society, and one into which society may look to correct its ills, it may well begin its work in the elementary classroom.

A sense of social values which characterizes a higher type of integration should be transmitted to the young child. All fields in education, in their own way, have within them this possibility. Plato[7] in his emphasis upon the importance of gymnastics and music, for example, does not refer to gymnastics as "physical exercise" and music as a "subject" but rather to these as a means of developing "a mind which is truly well made in its inner being." The development of such minds he regards as of utmost importance to society.

Art education, in its concern with unity of material, form, and content, its concern with developing an adequate seeing, imagination, and intuition, is one means of conveying to the child an idea of a "logico-meaningful unity." Through the use of art materials school children may grasp the meaning of unity. Trained to express in art materials their unified and meaningful reactions to the world about them, young children are given a common core of understanding which unites them in that it provides them with a means of communication and appreciation. With art materials "unity" can be "diagrammed," as it were.

The emphasis, then, that meaningful art education places on unity is the basis of its claim to social value, for unity in its highest form is essential for a better society. For this very reason, the other methods of art education mentioned in Chapter I, namely the Directing method, the Free-expression method, and the Eclectic method, may be questioned for their social value.

The Directing method seems to be characterized by a "spatial adjacency" of elements.

The Free-expression method as described also may fall short (due to its lack of conscious purpose) of characteristics of the higher types of integration.

The Eclectic method, of course, shares the characteristics of the first two.

SUMMARY

A Meaningful art education recognizes that there is a relationship between art and society and only as its efforts are exerted toward the higher integrating characteristics of art will it have unifying effect upon society.

The principles that have been set forth here will be further explained, in terms of their practical application in the classroom, in the chapter that follows.

REFERENCE BOOKS, CHAPTER IV

[1]Sorokin, P. A., *The Crisis of Our Age*. New York: E. P. Dutton Co., Inc., 1942. p. 30.

[2]Sorokin, P. A., *Social and Cultural Dynamics,* Vol. I. Fluctuations of Forms of Art. New York: American Book Co., 1937. pp. 10-19.

[3]*Op. cit.,* Sorokin, *The Crisis of Our Age.* pp. 16-17.

[4]Ulich, Robert, *Conditions of Civilized Living.* New York: E. P. Dutton and Co., Inc., 1946. p. 244.

[5]Dewey, John, *Problems of Men.* New York: Philosophical Library, 1946. pp. 26-27.

[6]Mumford, Lewis, *The Condition of Man.* New York: Harcourt, Brace and Co., 1944. p. 415.

[7]Plato's *Republic,* Book III, I. A. Richards Translation. New York: W. W. Norton and Co., Inc., 1942. p. 65.

CHAPTER V

Basic Postulates for a
Meaningful Art Education

THE PRINCIPLES that have been set forth in the preceding chapters may be interpreted into art practice in the school classroom. Esthetic, individual, and social values which are the concern of a Meaningful art education must in some way be conveyed to the child. Since none of these values is of a tangible nature, it is immediately evident that a method concerned with their transfer shall be one of *guidance* rather than one of *direction*. In this connection it might be well to refer to the words of Gibran in *The Prophet*:

"No man can reveal to you ought but that which already lies half asleep in the dawning of your knowledge."

First, in considering esthetic values in relation to practice in the school, it is interesting to note the resemblance of the "three kinds of beauty," mentioned

2. The Manipulative stage. The young child enjoys daubing
paint on a paper. Here begins his understanding of material.
No artist can produce "the sensuous beauty of material"
(first esthetic category) without love for that material. (Referred to on page 101.)

3. The Form-experimental stage. "The formal beauty of the design" (second esthetic category) is evident in the work of every normal child who is allowed natural development. (Referred to on page 102.)

4. The Early-expressive stage. "The expressive beauty of meaning" (third esthetic category) typifies the emphatic expression of the young child. (Referred to on page 102.)

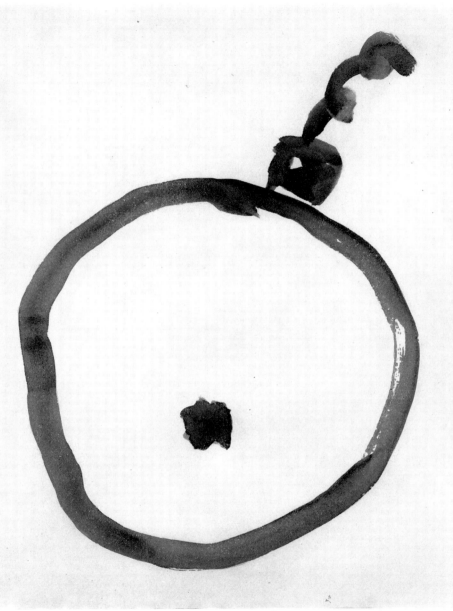

5. "House With Me Inside." Typical of the Early-expressive
stage when children still depict their empathic reactions to
their surroundings. (Referred to on page 103.)

6. "Wave Going Over Me." Typical of the Early-expressive stage when children still depict their empathic reactions to their surroundings. (Referred to on page 103.)

7. "House-Tree-Sun Picture." Typical stereotype which children produce when their empathic expressions are not understood and accepted. (Referred to on page 105.)

8. "Rabbit, Tulip, and Pumpkin on Fence." Drawing lesson clichés which end art as a means of expression. The integrity of the child's intention as evidenced in earlier productions has not been extended and developed. Instead blind procedures are required of the child. (Referred to on page 105.)

9. "Octopus," by eight-year-old. Organization of form and color combine with the study of marine life. (Referred to on page 135.)

in Chapter II, to three typical stages through which young children pass if they are given art materials and encouraged to use then intently. These stages, not necessarily successive, may be described as a Manipulative stage,*[1] a Form-experimental stage,† and an Early Expressive stage.†

EARLY "STAGES" OF VISUAL EXPRESSION

In the first or *manipulative stage,* page 85, the child not only familiarizes himself with the material but seems to derive genuine pleasure from the handling of it. The necessity of this stage is not limited to the young child. Adults, too, require a period of experimentation when they use materials for the first time. For example, if an adult sets out to paint a piece of furniture he is quite likely to try out the paint and the brush on a board before he applies it to the piece to be finished. He needs familiarity with both the materials and the tools before he can use them effectively. The period of manipulation for the young child, painting for the first time, may find him making what seem to be meaningless daubs for several months. Teachers closely associated with very young children have observed within the manipulative stage a steady im-

---

*This term is used by Margaret Mathias in *The Beginning of Art in the Public Schools.*

†These terms are the writer's, chosen because of their apparent relationship to the artistic categories.

provement in control of the material and a gradual transition into a more advanced stage, a form-experimental stage.

In the *form-experimental stage,* page 87, as in the manipulative stage, there is no apparent intention to name what is painted, but here there seems to be rather definite purpose as far as organizing forms is concerned. More frequently than not, children who have been allowed natural development up to this point are able to balance and unify masses of color.

When the child reaches the third stage, the *early expressive stage**, page 89, he begins to name the objects in his painting. Because of the fragmentary nature of the pictures in this stage the objects are often unrecognizable until they are explained by the child himself. Sometimes symbols are used in this stage — that is, signs that have little of the physical characteristics of the object. Frequently, however, what is understood by the observer to be a "symbol" is, in reality, a fragmentary illustration of the object, or of the feeling that the child may have toward the object.

---

*The *early expressive stage* is called the "symbolic stage" by some writers. Because *symbol* may mean a sign having little of the physical characteristics of the object (as a dollar sign standing for money), it seems better to use the broader term *early expressive,* which may include this narrow meaning of symbol as well as the fragmentary illustration of the object or of the feeling toward the object. If the broader meaning of symbol were always understood this change would not be necessary.

The drawing of a house (see illustration, page 91) appears at first glance to be a symbol having little relationship to the physical characteristics of a house.

The young child draws a circle and says, "There is a house." Then he places a dot within the circle and says, "This is me inside."

From the point of view of vision alone there is little resemblance to a house with a child in it, but considered in the sense of the child's empathic feeling toward a house there is a resemblance. Here the child has expressed the walls that surround him; the place where he stands on the floor is a dot.

A similar example of this early fragmentary type of expression is shown in the illustration on page 93. The four-year-old says: "This is a wave going over me at the beach." The "wave going over me at the beach" shows an essential expressive quality of the wave, in a very fragmentary form, of course.

Permanent Value of Early Stages

It is a mistake to consider these three early stages as types of expression that may be left behind once the child begins to draw more recognizable objects. These three stages are the very basis of Santayana's three kinds of beauty. The sensuous beauty of the material is often quite evident in early manipulative painting and clay modeling. The child loves the material and his handling of it is natural. The sensitivity the child has for the material at this early age should be developed further and carried through all of the child's work.

The natural feeling the child shows for balance and organization of form in the form-experimental stage is immediately recognizable as the beginning of a feeling for the formal beauty of the design, and, as such, every effort should be made to preserve and develop it.

In the early expressive stage the attempt to express "the house" or "the wave going over my head" is in nucleus the same kind of *empathic* expression that is found in great masterpieces of art such as *Pieta* by El Greco. Such feeling by the child should not receive correction based on shallow surface notions of how an object should look. Instead the child should be encouraged to develop such attempts into more complete and perhaps more deliberate and conscious expression. He should be guided to further expression in which he always retains the integrity of his intentions.

Unfortunately, the moment the child reaches the early expressive stage, it is almost inevitable that someone — teacher, parent, or another child — gives him a few static patterns that end art as a genuine means of expression. Instead of his being encouraged to develop further his own meaningful expression, the child who has painted his conception of a house is told, "No, that is not a house; this is a house," and the typical, rectangular, pitched-roof house so familiar to everyone is drawn for him. He is provided at that moment with a static picture that ends art creativity for a great many children.

The House-Tree-Sun-Sky-Grass Habit

The picture is a familiar one with few variations. Generally it is comprised of a house, tree, sun, sky, at the top, grass at the bottom. It is so typical that it cannot be ignored here. It appears even in those schools where every effort is made to preserve the more natural attempts at art expression.

It is somewhat paradoxical that early concern on the part of the teacher with what has seemed to him to be the child's inability to draw fades once the child has lost the qualities of the three early stages and in their place is only the picture shown in illustration 7, which the child draws over and over again. It is here that many a teacher decides that art ability is a gift which few people have. At this point children are stopped in their art development. Classroom teachers are puzzled as how to proceed to have their pupils develop beyond the "house-tree-sun" stage.

The directing method attempts to solve the problems by adding more static forms to the child's "repertoire." The tulip, the pumpkin on the fence, and the rabbit are notable examples. See illustration 8.

It is quite as unreasonable to expect a child to build facility in art expression by the addition of such static objects as it would be to attempt to build his language with a set of definite sentences which he does not understand.

Such forms as the "tulip" and the "rabbit" have no expressive meaning for the child. The fact that they are given to the child indicates an impatience on the part of the adult, due probably to the lack of understanding of the value of the early developmental stages in art.

"READINESS" FOR VISUAL EXPRESSION

In art expression as in other areas of learning, readiness for more advanced stages of learning is necessary before such learning can take place. Just as certain understandings and concepts are prerequisite to, and an essential part of, learning to read, so certain early practices in art, however elementary they seem to the adult, are prerequisite to, and part of, art expression.

The doctrine of readiness, however, according to Burton, is subject to misinterpretation.

"We are led to think of 'readiness' as a definite locus or condition. This leads to three subsidiary errors: (a) neglect of the genetic development of any power, skill, or understanding; (b) waiting for the given condition to appear of itself; (c) assuming without investigation that readiness must be present."[2] He adds that such errors cause the teacher to overlook the importance of "stimulation, opportunity, and tryout."

The problem of finding just the right point for stimulating the child to further learning is an important one.

In regard to art, it seems generally that while the child is in the first two stages and until he is well into the early expressive stage he requires little if any reference to idea or subject matter. Up to this time he is content and eager to experiment with materials. While this interest is still strong, suggestion that the child depict some specific idea or experience may assume without sufficient evidence, "that readiness must be present." To avoid this, it is well to be cautious and to place emphasis not on pushing the child into making more recognizable pictures but rather on the forming of good working habits — the proper handling and care of brushes, and, as much as possible, the keeping of paint from clothing and the floor. Of course, encouragement and approval of the child's early efforts are always of utmost importance. The teacher is always alert to the progress the child makes and ready to recognize his emergence into a more advanced stage when he may need more specific suggestions, or focus, in regard to idea or subject matter for his painting. Such an attitude is not, as Burton says, one of "waiting for the given condition to appear of itself," for it should

take into consideration fully the importance of "stimulation, opportunity, and tryout," but such stimulation
should be on a level appropriate to the child's present
stage of development.

When the child is well into the early expressive
stage his interest in materials, as such, no longer holds
him to continued activity as was the case in the two
earlier stages. At this time(except in rare cases), unless the teacher takes an active part in providing the
conditions for producing expression and recognizing
expression once it has occurred, only a few children
will continue to use art as a means of expression. It is
in the early expressive stage, as was mentioned above,
that the house-tree-sun picture is likely to appear, and
unless the teacher has definite procedures to counteract
this "static picture" little progress may be made beyond it.

STIMULATION AND EVALUATION OF MEANINGFUL ART CREATIVITY

In order to stimulate meaningful art creativity, it
is important (1)*that the child have something to express*, (2) *that the child be made aware of the possibility of expressing his ideas and feelings in art materials*, and (3) *that he be helped to understand, enjoy,
and appreciate the materials, organization, and the
meaning of his work and the work of others*. The unity
of means and end, process and product, in the child's

10. "Lions." Anatomy of creature is grasped as a whole rather than through analysis; by ten-year-old child. (Referred to on page 135.)

11. "Wild Horses." The twelve-year-old, while painting this picture, pretended he was a horse himself and "galloped" as he
turned from his paint jars to the paper that was taped to the
blackboard. (Referred to on page 137.)

early creative attempts depends upon these three conditions.

The first point — *the child must have something to express* — is dependent upon experience. Only the person who experiences richly has something to intuit or express. Experience, in turn, depends upon developed powers of observation and imagination. Development of observation or awareness of the elements and relationships in one's environment is fundamental to education. Observation is more than a physical or mechanical process. One of the fallacies of a directing method is the assumption that everyone sees exactly the same thing in a given area at all times. Visual experiments at The Princeton Institute in Hanover, N. H., point out that this is not the case and that what each individual sees is determined by his experience and his purposes.

In asking the child to draw or paint a picture that he, not the child, visualizes, the teacher makes an impossible demand and retards rather than promotes the development of the child's powers of observation, for the environment of two persons may be similar but never identical. Seeing, moreover, is a selective rather than a mechanical process.

Instead of the child's being asked to portray the teacher's world, he should be guided to portray his own. The teacher and the child have something in common. But this something does not lie in the specific surface aspects of a visual world but in the power to comprehend the inner structure of matter, form, and content. The outward expression is the unique contribution of the individual expressing, which serves only as a conveyance of an idea, an idea that can be grasped because there is some identity between the nature of the one expressing and the one receiving the communication. You do not say to the child, "Observe this!" but rather, "What do you observe?"

Imagination is the faculty of constructing relationships in both space and time; therefore it is closely linked to observation. There would be no observation without imagination. Imagination like intuition (see page 48) has its roots in experience, but through it new linkages and meanings are formulated. It provides a continuous renewal of the individual's relationships to an ever changing world.

Imagination serves a purpose other than that of discovering relationships in the space-time world. It enables the individual to have vicarious as well as actual experience. In art education, as in other fields, vicarious as well as actual experience is important.

"Few of us will be fortunate enough to 'experience' directly the delta of the Nile, the geography of India, the contents of the world's art galleries, the life of the Nomads of Asia Minor. Futhermore, no one can experience four thousand years of history, nor the actual life of Shakespeare, nor the crossing of the Rubicon. A vivid and reasonably complete vicarious experience with Caesar may contribute, however, to the ability to cross one's own Rubicons as they appear in life."[3]

Vicarious or imaginary experience is valuable not only as an addition to actual experience but also in that it may provide, without actual change of environment, the contrast or variety necessary to make one aware of the possibilities and limitations of his actual environment. In other words it facilitates and supports observation.

Alfred North Whitehead in *Process and Reality* states, "We habitually observe by the method of difference.... when the method of difference fails, factors which are constantly present may yet be observed under the influence of imaginative thought. Such thought supplies the differences which the direct observation lacks."[4]

In providing experience for the child it is important to recognize the value of contrast and change.

As is implied above, it is not only physical change of location that may provide the necessary contrasts to an otherwise humdrum existence, the imaginary land of the story book provides a journey that presents many and varied experiences. A trip across Africa with *The Elephant's Child* gives much material for art expression and the tangible expression further enlivens the experience. The imaginary journey, by contrast to the monotony of the classroom, sharpens the sensibilities of the young artist, and he sets about eagerly to objectify in paint his new and vivid "experience" in the land of animal and jungle.

Just as the change brought about by his flight into the imaginary world of story has a vitalizing effect, so his "return" to what was before a drab and monotonous classroom now by contrast takes on a new brightness, that in his closeness it did not possess. Such is the value of developing the imagination.

Without the contrasts that are brought about by change, it is doubtful if art expression would take place because there would be insufficient experience to stimulate expression. The individual would become dull and indifferent to his surroundings.

As imagination develops, the need for strongly contrasting change lessens. The young artist with a developed imagination sees the vivid aspects of everyday environment that would be non-existent for an undeveloped imagination.

Not only is the interdependence of actual and imaginary experience important in developing awareness to one's surroundings, but the objectification or problem solving of such experience is equally essential. The child intent upon painting a picture of his "trip" through Africa finds it no passive journey. The words of the story are transposed into vivid mental pictures which, in turn, his brush and paint objectify.

The increased awareness of the child to his surroundings, brought about by the interchange of imaginary and actual experience plus the objectification of
that experience, may contribute not only to his capacity for art expression, but may be in itself a valuable
contribution to the child's total educational development. Certainly to be alert to one's environment is
important to the well-being of the individual. As art
practice contributes to the development of this alert-
ness to environment, it has a general educational value.

It is well known that many a prisoner of World
War II retained his mental and physical health by
proper use of imagination. Life in the prison camp
was monotonous and seemingly hopeless. There was
little or no hope of actual change of environment. A
prisoner of six years tells how painting, play acting,
and music provided the necessary change from the
humdrum routine of his daily existence. Part of the
time he had to face the reality of the prison camp
but outside of working hours he and others created
for themselves through imagination another world —
a world of color, of order, and of music. In the short
interval of such flights of the imagination he and others
were able to renew their vigor and restore their hope
and see new possibilities in their future. It must be
emphasized, however, that it is a balance of actual and
vicarious experience that is needed, for to live continuously in a world of fantasy would be quite as harm-

ful as facing the reality of prison life without relief.

It is this balance that should be sought in the school classroom. If a child were required to work on painting all day, each day, he would become as dull as if he were required to work continuously on arithmetic and spelling. Visual expression, music, drama, physical activity *properly spaced* in the program to meet needs for contrast and change not only make happier, healthier children but facilitate other learning.

Stories, actual experience, subject matter from social studies provide excellent material for art expression for the child, but *all* stories, actual experiences, or subject matter of social studies may not lend themselves to art expression. Just as some of the events of our lives call for no verbal comment, many experiences, imaginary or actual, do not call for visual expression. Considerable disregard for this principle is frequently seen in an attempt to "correlate" social studies with art.

When the subject matter of the social studies is developed to a point where the child may formulate clear mental pictures of the particular event or situation, it may be material for art expression. In turn, such expression is valuable to the social studies in that such objectification of the subject matter tends to intensify and clarify the particular event or situation. However, such productions should be evaluated for their artistic qualities as is any other art work.

It is questionable if copying pictures from history or geography books, as is often done in relation to the social studies, is of value in building genuine experience for the child. If pictures are wanted to illustrate some factual aspect of the social studies or some characteristic of a documentary nature, rather than make copied drawings it is better to refer to the original photograph and let it go at that.

Visual aid materials are most helpful in teaching many subjects; they are of service to art only as they build vivid concepts of the object or event, but not as models to be imitated. Pictures serve an important role in enlarging the child's experience and in helping him build concepts of objects he has no opportunity to see in the original; but pictures or photographs used in immediate connection with art expression are more likely to serve as a block than as an aid to genuine art expression.

Reference to pictures while the child is trying to draw serves as a block to expression because it removes a very important factor necessary to the development of observation — *the necessity of problem solving.*

When the child becomes discouraged at his first attempt to draw an object, to allow him to refer to a picture to solve his problem is comparable in the literary field to giving him stock sentences to use in writing a composition. In either case, need for further thinking and observation is eliminated because a final solution, and quite a superficial one, has been given.

It is desirable that the child does not have *complete* satisfaction with his earliest attempts at expression, for it is only when the need for improvement is felt that it is likely to be made. On the other hand, it is important that the child have some feeling of success, for a sense of complete failure might be quite as fatal to further progress as a feeling of complete success.

Procedure that takes into consideration the importance of problem solving might be as follows:

The importance of vivid subject matter has been emphasized above as a prerequisite of art expression. The child whose art expression is blocked with the "house-tree-sun" picture is stimulated to a new expression by a vivid story, or by calling of attention to the possibility of expressing some event in his actual experience.

His first attempt to express specific objects or ideas may not satisfy him, and the natural tendency is for him to want the problem solved at once by teacher assistance or by reference to pictures. Such an immediate solution to his problem relieves the necessity of further observation, and does not build the basic and organic elements of art expression or develop a more adequate seeing.

The results of the first attempt the child makes to express his ideas in art materials may be fragmentary, but they may represent his understanding and

12. "The bottom-of-the-page" picture. Qualities of the three
early stages have disappeared. Discouragement and dislike
for drawing are inevitable unless feeling for material form
and content can be recaptured. (Referred to on page 140.)

13. "The Clown," by an eight-year-old. Early realization of both two and three dimensional space. There is grass behind the boy and "grouping." The hut is behind the clown. Things "fit" too. (Referred to on page 151.)

14. "Water Buffalo Surrounded by Hunters" by a twelve-year-old. The idea here helped produce "figures going in all directions." (Referred to on page 153.)

15. "Old Frank's Death Bed." A week before this picture was painted "Old Frank," beloved by all the children, died in the Buffalo Zoo. The twelve-year-old explained, "That's the zoo keeper scratching his head while the veterinary can't do a thing." (Referred to on page 153.)

16. "Madonna." "Mary looks saintly" was the comment of a
third grader when his eight-year-old classmate produced this
picture. (Referred to on page 173.)

17. "Christmas Mural." Seventy-eight different children from grades 1-8 worked on this large mural. The familiar theme and the idea "Make things fit." (Referred to on page 175.)

observations of that particular moment. To repeat,
some feeling of dissatisfaction with his picture (his
hypothesis of the object at that moment) may be an
essential drive to further observation. A child who
attempts to draw a horse to the best of his ability,
and finds that in the process he does not have sufficient
knowledge of a horse, does not have to be told to look
more closely at a horse the next time he sees one. In
retrospect to his struggle to express a horse, the actual
presence of the animal takes on a new meaning. In
his first attempt at drawing, perhaps he could not
visualize the direction in which the horse's legs bend,
although he had seen a horse many times. Until he
had the need that was occasioned by his attempt to
draw it there was no reason for making so close an observation. Once the attempt to draw the horse is made,
the need for greater observation is felt. Many repe-
titions of such a pattern of observation, hypothesis, and
further observation, increase the child's power of observation and consequently of expression.

The second point of importance in teaching art is
*that the child must be made aware of the possibility
of expressing his ideas and feeling in art materials.*
In most cases the child's attention must be called to
the fact that his experiences may be expressed visually.
Some teachers of English encourage their students to
develop "the daily theme eye." In other words, they
call the attention of the student to commonplace events

that may be valuable subject material for writing. In art, it is important that the teacher be alert to the things the child might express, and suggest that he do so; the child is encouraged to develop the "daily picture eye." Once the child forms the practice of expressing the seemingly commonplace events of his everyday life, one of the most important steps in art expression — that of having something to say — is achieved.

Not only should children's attention be called to the fact that their imaginary or remembered experiences may be expressed in art materials, but they may (in the intermediate grades in the elementary school, rarely before) be encouraged to work from actual models, people, animals, and landscapes. In this connection sometimes the question is asked, and rightly so, "What is the difference between copying a picture and copying a model?" If no interpretation of the model is made, there is essentially no difference, except that the problem of drawing a three-dimensional object on a two-dimensional paper is not already solved. But since art expression involves a different kind of seeing, it aims not to depict an objective view of the object, but to interpret the object esthetically and, therefore, expressively.

To produce in one's painting the *three qualities of beauty* it is necessary to see them in the model, be it life, landscape, imagined scene or activity. The *artist* "copies" what he "sees," but he sees through the eyes of an artist.

Here one is brought face to face with those intangibles of art expression that require the individual to move from perception to apperception. It is here that art expression must become more than a form of practice or random activity. The *artist* preserves the vision that the young child has before the

> Shades of the prison-house begin to close
> Upon the growing boy.

The very young child, as if by instinct, seems to balance the masses and colors in his pictures. See illustration 9, page 99. A little later he is able to catch and express the spirit of a live creature or natural scene without an analytical knowledge of what he expresses. See illustration 10, page 109.

But the power to continue to express such a synthesis, as is shown in these illustrations, seems to disappear unless the child develops apperception, unless he *becomes consciously aware of his intuitive powers.* Perhaps the greatest problem of art education is how to help the child make the transition from the seemingly non-self-conscious expression to the self-conscious expression. As was said above, most children must be made aware through suggestion that their experiences are material for visual expression. Now it is necessary to guide the child to seek consciously and deliberately the formal and meaningful organization in the world about him.

The old rules of design — balance, rhythm, harmony, repetition, and dominance, etc. — have failed to produce a genuine synthesis of material, form, and content. These rules, like insistence upon anatomical proportion and mechanical perspective, may produce a pleasing "spatial adjacency" of objects but rarely a spirited integration of material, form, and content that typifies great art throughout the centuries. A substitute for these old rules of design is necessary. "Make things fit" seems to be a term which children readily understand. They soon learn that lines, masses, colors, dark and light, size and shape "fit" if they are pleasing to the eye.

"What is pleasing to the eye?" one may ask. The only answer we can give is that most human beings desire some kind of unity or balance. Most people know that a limb from an apple tree would not look well on a weeping willow or vice-versa.

One of the outstanding problems in art teaching lies in the fact that learning is in part dependent upon teacher approval. This brings us to the third point, that *recognition and evaluation of the child's expressions are important*. As was said above, the child should be helped to understand, enjoy, and appreciate the material, the organization, and the meaning of his work. The child soon learns what kind of work is acceptable to the teacher. If the child is to learn to express in an organized manner, the teacher must have the ability to recognize such expression when it occurs. This requires artistically intuitive insight on the part of the teacher.

Unless the teacher has become sensitive to expressive form, he is likely to make judgments of children's work that go no deeper than personal likes and dislikes. Approval based simply on the teacher's preference can serve no artistic purpose. It is important, then, in attempting to foster art expression in the child, that the teacher develop in himself an artistically intuitive sense.

A teacher having a well-developed artistic sense is more likely to realize the caution that is necessary in evaluating children's works. He makes no attempt to draw sharp lines of demarcation between "good" and "bad," and yet he senses that subtle balance, that "just rightness" when it appears in a child's work and quietly approves.

The twelve-year-old child who drew the horses, illustration 11, said one day, "I always try to be not too tight, not too sloppy, but just right."

There is no formula for "just rightness" and yet it is not a product of simple personal preference. It goes deeper into human experience: it has an element of universality about it; it is *intuition*.

Attempt has been made to show that art expression

having the "three kinds of beauty" may not be measured objectively. Such expression depends upon an inner feeling for organization and unity.

It is no more practical to attempt to teach and to measure art by formula than it is to attempt to teach a person to ride a bicycle by dictating exactly how far the handlebars must be turned to right or left to keep the bicycle in equilibrium. Indeed, some mathematician might produce a formula for this, but for practical purposes it would be useless because of the infinite number of variations that would be necessary.

In learning to ride the bicycle the child makes attempts and hits upon the proper balance, which in this case is easily recognized.

In drawing, on the other hand, he may "accidentally" draw an expressive and organized picture, but unless it is recognized and approved it is doubtful if he will "learn" to make such pictures — that is, be able to do so repeatedly.

When right and wrong cannot be well defined, as is the case in art, the necessary dependence upon teacher approval presents a problem. Both "good" and "bad" ways of working may be learned, to some extent depending upon the sensitivity and understanding of the teacher. This same problem, however, exists in all areas where learning is other than factual. The parent who attempts to train the child to good behavior must risk making mistakes because of the relative nature of good behavior. There is always a temptation, because of the danger of making a mistake in this connection, of setting up absolute rules and by rationalization convincing oneself that adherence to those rules is all that is necessary to be right.

Such a procedure is likely to result in the wrong kind of learning, as when standards have as their only basis a sense of values. The choice of absolute rules is originally a subjective one, and, therefore, subject to the same errors as is a dependence upon a sense of values. Realizing this problem, the only course for a teacher of art is to discover as far as is possible the values that seem inherent in the subject, and to proceed with the utmost caution in approving the child's effort on the basis of these values.

In any subject, a teacher must know to the best of his ability the characteristics of that subject, for he has entrusted to him the right to approve or disapprove the work of others.

EVALUATION OF CHILDREN'S WORK

At this point it is important to offer a few practical suggestions for criticising children's work. They are by no means complete and final in any way. They are offered as suggestions for giving the child guidance to meaningful organized expression.

When children are first encouraged to draw other

than the house-tree-sun picture they frequently draw very small objects on the bottom of the page, with little concern for the relationship of one figure to another or of the figures to the page. See illustration 12.

Perhaps the teacher has told a story as a means of providing experience from which the child may draw. In the resulting picture the sky is represented by a strip of blue at the top of the paper and the grass by a strip of green at the bottom. The habitual drawing of the sun cannot be resisted. The tree and the house are inevitably present too. There are few compliments possible for the picture, but the teacher tries to find what good might exist in it.

The next time the children draw, however, the teacher tells them, "Remember how tiny our figures were last week? They were little and right down on the bottom of the page. Today let's make our figures keep up from the bottom of the page; make them large, as large as our arm, and fill the page."

The child's picture then is evaluated on whether or not he has related object to his page. The teacher is not concerned with anatomical proportion, for he knows that development of empathic seeing will result in esthetic proportion and it is with the latter of course that art is mainly concerned. To demand anatomical proportions not only presents a task too difficult for the young child and therefore discourages him, but also prevents the development of empathic seeing.

18. "The Houses Next Door." A painting by a twelve-year-old
girl made from her window.

19. "Vultures in the Desert," by an eleven-year-old.

20. "The Elephant's Burying Ground," by a twelve-year-old. Not analysis but an imaginative grasp for the whole can produce such an organized relationship.

21. "Hungry Alligators," by an eight-year-old.

The child must have some feeling of success, however. It is within his power to keep figures up from the bottom of the page, to work large, and to fill the page, and since these three suggestions lead to a better sense of the materials and of organization, they are justifiable as a way of progress. If the picture fulfills the above requirements, it is accepted and approved by the teacher. These suggestions are made, not because they are all-important in themselves, but because they, in an indirect way, lead the child to a greater realization of the materials, spatial relationship, and expressive quality.

There is an objection to the emphasis that is placed on encouraging children to make large figures. If this emphasis is based on some notion that large figures, as such, are esthetically better than small ones, the objection is a justifiable one. It is also justifiable on another point. The size in which a person draws is a personal matter and should be determined by individual reactions and preferences. These two objections, however, do not change the necessity of encouraging the young child to draw large figures. The possibility of composing the whole page is easier by using few large figures rather than many small ones. After the child senses the importance of relationship of figures to the dimension of the paper he may make them small or large as he wishes.

In reference to the desirability of the child's establishing his own individual size, it should be understood that frequently the small drawing he makes is not a product of his individual preference, but very often an imitation of the drawing by others. Someone may have shown him how to draw with a pencil on a very small piece of paper, thus establishing a small size that is not natural to him; or he may have developed restricted finger movement while learning to write. Showing the child that he can work large as well as small might help him to establish the size most natural to himself and at the same time develop greater control of materials through freedom of movement.

Another reason for encouraging young children to work large is that their small muscles necessary for more detailed movements are not developed. Larger and less detailed movements are accompanied by the possibility of greater control. As the child gets older and his smaller muscles develop, he may be able to refine these large movements into more detailed ones.

Free bodily movement is as necessary to expresive painting as it is to expressive dancing. The more detailed and intricate movements are a refinement of the larger ones — not a painful cramping for effect — before muscular development allows the greater control.

After the child has drawn many examples fulfilling the first three requirements and his drawing takes on more detail, it is time to go a step further. To this point he has attempted no three-dimensional drawing.

The introduction to three-dimensional drawing is made quite easily by reference to the grass strip at the bottom of the page.

"Why don't you put some grass behind the boy as well as in front of him?" He learns that putting the grass up higher makes the grass behind the boy. See illustration 13.

Later he learns to "group." He can put the house back on the grass that is behind the boy. Along with the idea of grouping he is encouraged to "make things fit." Then he is encouraged to turn figures in many directions. Of course, all of this time he is using color and is encouraged to make some things dark and some things light. He also learns that there are many tones of one color and that he can mix colors to get these tones. Instead of learning how to mix color in a rote way, that "yellow and blue make green," he learns to see yellow and blue in green.

These steps here are given in somewhat logical order. The teacher sould use in *not* so logical order!

1. Keep figures up from the bottom of page.
2. Work large.
3. Fill the page.
4. Group figures and objects.
5. Make things "fit."
6. Make figures go in all directions and take many positions.

7. Make some things light and some things dark.
8. Balance a color with another tone of the color.
9. *Mean* what you paint.

Nothing could hamper the school art program more than to attempt to teach a class in unison the above steps. Art teaching is an *individual* matter and there will be many variations to these steps. They may provide a teacher with some basis of judgment that is not so definite and exacting that it crushes out all creativity, and yet one that may help to guide the child to organized and unified expression.

The personality of the teacher has much to do with what may be said to the child to foster meaningful creativity. The same words said by one teacher producing good results might produce quite opposite results if said by another. The art teacher armed with understanding of his field must have his finger on the pulse of the particular situation and act according to his better judgements, realizing fully the possibility of directing the child too much, or of allowing him to dissipate his energies.

The steps above, it will be noticed, refer to *general* rather than to specific characteristics of an art work. Attention of the child is called to broad formal and expressive aspects of what he is to draw or paint, rather than to the specific aspects such as correct anatomical proportion and correct mechanical perspective.

A method that is meant to develop in the child an

artistic sense must not dissect the very unity it hopes to emphasize.

Anatomical proportions and perspective may result in a work in which emphasis is placed upon analysis, but to direct the attention of little children to such details is likely to break their idea of the whole. Indications of anatomical proportions or perspective in the photographs of children's work shown here have resulted from what seemed to be an intuitive grasp of the total pattern of the object. No analysis of parts was encouraged by the teacher.

Illustration 14, "African Natives Surrounding a Water Buffalo," is an example of a work of a twelve-year-old child who knew no rules of mechanical perspective and could not say how many times greater the body is than the head. But within less than an hour he was able to paint this picture, directly in paint—that is, without a previous sketch. Had he been stopped in the process to worry about the direction the horns of the water buffalo should take, according to rules of perspective, it is doubtful if he could have in any way approximated the fine relationship these horns show to the body of the animal.

"The Dying Elephant," illustration 15, presents another example of an intuitive grasp of the total idea. The subject matter of both of these pictures was imaginary. No similar pictures were shown to the child.

On the elementary school level, analysis of proportion and perspective seems to retard rather than to promote the ability of the child to draw. If there is a need in art for such analysis, it is doubtful if it should be considered during the early years when art expression for the child is in a formative stage. Again, if a reference to language may be made — a child is not expected to understand the intricacies of grammar before he learns to talk, but it does not follow that he speaks ungrammatically until he is able to analyze his speech.

ART IN DAILY LIVING

While drawing and painting as a means of expression are specifically emphasized in this presentation, it is not intended that other areas are to be considered unimportant in the art program.

The average schoolroom with its formal and crowded seating arrangement in many cases limits the art program to drawing, painting, and some modeling. For practical reasons, then, emphasis is placed on what may be done and done to advantage in average school classrooms. Good teaching in painting and drawing is important in any case, for it may provide the child with considerable artistic sensitivity. Painting, drawing, and modeling, although they have values in their own right, should also serve as a springboard to practice in, and appreciation of, other artistic forms.

The principles involved in using materials sensitively, organizing form, and being concerned with meaning or function may apply to many aspects of the individual's activity. The arranging of a room, planting of a garden, preparing of a meal, painting of a picture — all may be based upon these principles. Art so considered may be truly a pervading element.

The child who learns to express in terms of these principles derives a personal satisfaction from his accomplishment. The standards that are set up in terms of the "steps" mentioned on page 151, although not absolute, provide the child with a basis for judging his own work as well as the work of his classmates. After a little training the child becomes less dependent upon the opinion of the teacher to decide the success of his efforts. The child learns for himself that his work is satisfying because he learns to recognize the importance of the unity which is characteristic of, and essential to, his own nature.

When the child has a grasp of esthetic qualities in his work, he has a basis for understanding the work of others who also have this fundamental approach to art. Then, no matter how different the experiences of each individual may be, here is a common ground, a possible meeting place for all children. The specific subject matter of one child's painting may be of little or no interest to another child whose experience may be quite different, but artistic quality, once it is sensed, provides a common meeting ground for both.

The skillful teacher knows the social value of a common ground on which all children may meet. The presence of such an element in some form is necessary for better social living. Sorokin says men are not united by their likenesses nor their differences but by the values they place upon these. Evaluation of the art work in the school is done by the children themselves under the guidance of the teacher. Before such evaluation may take place, the children must have some idea of what is expected of them in terms of some of the steps mentioned on page 151.

In the very beginning perhaps only the first two or three steps may be mentioned. The child shows his picture and tells about it if he wishes. The other children are trained to make constructive criticism on the basis of the steps mentioned. "The boy that Richard drew in his picture looks more like a monkey than a boy," says one honest critic. "Oh," says the teacher, "we are going to say only the good things about the pictures. Did Richard work large, keep figures up from the bottom of the page, and fill his page?" The children soon learn that saying the good things about others guarantees their own security when their turn comes to show their pictures, and they eagerly search for something good to say about the work of the other fellow.

In this connection it is important to help the child develop genuine powers of discrimination. Because he

22. "Charging Buffalo." "They are coming right at me," said
the highly imaginative, eleven-year-old boy painter.

23. "Zebras Grazing," by a ten-year-old boy.

24. "Carnival," by a thirteen-year-old girl.

25. "Runaway Horses," by a ten-year-old.

26. "Beavers Building Dam." Perspective a result of observation rather than mechanical knowledge.

27. "Valley Forge," by a twelve-year-old girl.

28. "Happy Gorilla Family," by a ten-year-old boy.

29. "The First Thanksgiving." Brush drawing by a twelve-year-old.

may not ridicule the other child does not mean he must give insincere praise; learning is hampered by either. Children may be trained to be perfectly honest in this respect and at the same time not indulge in the negative criticism that is devastating to the young child's desire to continue to use art as a means of expression.

Notice the painting of a Madonna and child by a seven-year-old, illustration 16. Almost any adult first viewing this painting is amused at the way the nose is drawn. The children in this group made no comment or sign of recognition of this particular detail. One child remarked that Mary looked "saintly" and the rest agreed. Sometimes expressive lines are misplaced as may have been the case in this picture. But it is safer to assume that there is a serious side of such expression than to risk correcting or ridiculing what may have been created reverently.

A spirit of fellowship may be developed in a classroom when children enjoy and appreciate each other's work. Even the child with the least skill may become a part of the classroom unity because he is able to show some nice colors in his picture or perhaps appreciate the good picture someone else made. "John made a good picture," says William. "He filled his page and made things fit." John is grateful for William's appreciation and understanding.

A classroom conducted according to the above

practices does not "star" one child to the envy of all the rest. The child who seems to show exceptional talent is appreciated by all of the others, but he also learns to appreciate any accomplishment and improvement of the least able in the group. The children learn to love a picture that has artistic qualities and they are glad when it is made by anyone.

GROUP WORK

The social value of a meaningful art education may have even further implications as related to group work on large projects. The painting of a mural may be offered as an example here. Unless some fundamental, unifying basis on which to organize a group project is present, it is questionable whether such a project promotes social integration or social disintegration. The subject matter of the proposed mural alone does not seem to provide a sufficiently common ground of agreement necessary to the harmonious cooperation of a creating group. This idea is in keeping with Sorokin's claim that inner values are necessary to a higher kind of integration.[5] If children have no idea of plastic and meaningful organization in their individual work it is next to impossible to expect them to have it in relation to the work of others. A mural that is attempted with concern for only subject matter results in an arrangement of individual pictures whose respective position is dictated by the teacher or by one talented child. Throughout the process of making such a mural, there is likely to be much painful and unwilling compromise, and the whole undertaking may be questioned as to either its esthetic individual or social value.

If group work is to have social value, children must have some appreciation of the work of others before they are set to the task of creating in collaboration with others. To have such appreciation, a common basis of judgement such as the artistic principles is necessary.

Children who know the practical meaning of "grouping" and "making things fit" do not go to the mural and draw an object isolated from those drawn by all the rest. "You know how you make things 'fit' in your own pictures," says the teacher. "When you work on the mural, you look at what other people have done before you make your contribution so what you add 'fits' with the rest."

Illustration 17 shows a large mural, 12' x 60', that was made by seventy-eight different children who had learned first to relate forms to one another. In this project children were quick to recognize the contribution of the child who related his work to what was done before and they were equally alert to the child who simply added his contribution oblivious of the work of all the others.

In group projects such as is described above, there

is a certain conformity necessary. From the social point of view the degree of conformity that is possible depends upon the general character of the situation. It is only when values of a more universal nature are mutually understood that two or more people can work together harmoniously.

SUMMARY

A Meaningful approach to art education serves to guide the child to develop a sensitivity to esthetic, individual, and social values. There is a recognition of what seems to be the child's innate tendency to express in terms of beauty of material, beauty of form, and beauty of meaning as is evidenced in three early natural stages of child art — the Manipulative stage, the Form-experimental stage, and the Early Expressive stage. Attempt is made to preserve the child's natural sensitivity to material, form, and meaning, and to develop it. In such an attempt it is essential that synthesis rather than analysis of parts in isolation be the basis of evaluation and criticism. Instead of criticizing minute and factual details of the child's work, attention is deliberately directed to formal qualities. In a genuine art synthesis detailed elements develop as a part of the whole; they are never considered as isolated parts but rather as integral elements.

The child is led to develop a sensitivity to material and form by being encouraged to "work large," "fill the page," "make things fit." He is encouraged to "mean" what he paints, but he cannot do so unless he has something to say. Therefore it is essential that he be provided with vivid and meaningful experience and that he be made aware that such experience may be expressed in plastic materials for communication to others. The child's creation must be unified both plastically and meaningfully if it is to be of integrative value to him. The teacher may guide the child to create a plastic and meaningful unity by allowing him freedom for emotion and reflection within an ideal.

Group activity to be of social value also must be guided rather than directed by the teacher. Just as the child may see in his own painting a relationship of one form to another and one meaning to another, so he may be guided to see the relationship of his own creation to that of his neighbor.

REFERENCE BOOKS, CHAPTER V

[1]Mathias, Margaret, *The Beginning of Art in the Public Schools.* New York: Charles Scribner's Sons, 1924. p. 6.

[2]Burton, W. H., *The Guidance of Learning Activities.* New York: D. Appleton-Century Co., 1944. p. 159.

[3]*Ibid.* p. 75.

[4]Whitehead, Alfred North, *Process and Reality.* New York: The Macmillan Co., 1936. p. 7.

[5]Sorokin, P. A., *Social and Cultural Dynamics.* New York: American Book Co., 1937. pp. 18-19.

Bibliography

A Cyclopedia of Education, Paul Monroe, Editor, New York: The Macmillan Co., 1911. Vol. I.

Allport, Gordon, *Personality*. New York: Henry Holt and Co., 1937.

Art in American Life and Education. Fortieth Yearbook of the National Society for the Study of Education. Bloomington, Ill.: Public School Publishing Co., 1941.

Barnes, Albert C., *The Art in Painting*. New York: Harcourt, Brace and Co., 1937.

Barnes, Harry E., and Becker, Howard, *Social Thought From Lore to Science*. Boston, Mass.: D. C. Heath and Co.

Bell, Clive, *Art*. London: Chatto and Windus, 1920.

Binyon, Laurence, *The Flight of the Dragon*. London: John Murray, Albemarle Street, 1943.

Buermeyer, Laurence, *The Aesthetic Experience*. Merion, Pa.: The Barnes Foundation Press, 1929.

Burton, William H., *The Guidance of Learning Activities*. New York: D. Appleton-Century Co., 1944.

................, *The Guidance of Major Specialized Learning Activities Within the Total Learning Activity*. Cambridge, Mass.: Published by the Author, 1944.

Cheney, Sheldon, *A World History of Art*. New York: The Viking Press, 1937.

................, *A Primer of Modern Art*. New York: Boni and Liveright, 1924.

................, *Expression in Art*. New York: Liveright, 1934.

Circle, J. L. Martin, B. Nicholson, and N. Babo, Editors. London: Faber and Faber, 1937.

Cole, Natalie R., *The Arts in the Classroom*. New York: The John Day Co., 1940.

Coomaraswamy, Ananda, *Figures of Speech or Figures of Thought*. London: Luzar and Company, 1946.

Coomaraswamy, Ananda, *The Transformation of Nature in Art*. Cambridge, Mass.: Harvard University Press, 1934.

Creative Expression, Edited for the Progressive Education by Gertrude Hartman and Ann Schumaker. New York: The John Day Co., 1931.

Croce, Benedetto, *Aesthetic*. London: Macmillan and Co., 1922.

D'Amico, Victor, *Creative Teaching in Art*. Scranton, Pa.: International Textbook Co., 1941.

Danz, Louis, *The Psychologist Looks at Art*. New York: Longmans, Green and Co., 1937.

Dewey, John, *Art as Experience*. New York: G. P. Putnam's Sons, 1934.

Dewey, John; Barnes, Albert; and Others, *Art and Education*. Merion, Pa.: Barnes Foundation Press, 1929.

Dewey, John, *Problems of Men*. New York: Philosophical Library, 1946.

...................., *The Quest for Certainty*. New York: Minton, Balch and Co., 1929.

Dorner, Alexander, *The Way Beyond Art*. New York: Witterborn, 1947.

Edman, Irwin, *Arts and the Man*. New York: W. W. Norton and Co., 1939.

Flugel, J. C., *Man, Morals, and Society*. London: Duckworth, 1945.

Fry, Roger, *Last Lectures*. New York: The Macmillan Co., 1939.

...................., *Vision and Design*. New York: Coward-McCann, Inc., 1924.

Gilbert, Katherine, *A History of Aesthetics*. New York: The Macmillan Co., 1939.

...................., *Studies in Recent Aesthetics*. Chapel Hill, N. C.: The University of North Carolina Press, 1927.

Goldstein, H. and V., *Art in Everyday Life*. New York: The Macmillan Co., 1926.

Greene, Theodore, *The Arts and the Art of Criticism*. Princeton, N. J.: Princeton University Press, 1940.

Gropius, Walter, *The New Architecture and the Bauhaus*. New York: Museum of Modern Art, 1937.

Henri, Robert, *The Art Spirit*. New York: J. B. Lippincott Co., 1930.

Hildebrand, Adolf, *The Problem of Form in Painting and Sculpture*. New York: G. E. Stechert and Co., 1945.

Hiler, Hilaire, *Why Abstract?* Norfolk, Conn.: New Directions, 1945.

Hopkins, L. Thomas, *Integration*. New York: D. Appleton-Century Co., 1937.

Johnson, Wendel, *People in Quanderies*. New York: Harper, 1946.

Kandinsky, Wassily, *The Art of Spiritual Harmony*. London: Constable and Co., 1914.

Kepes, Gyorgy, *The Language of Vision*. Chicago: P. Theobald, 1944.

Lowenfeld, Viktor, *Creative and Mental Growth*. New York: Macmillan Co., Inc., 1947.

Mathias, Margaret, *The Beginning of Art in the Public Schools*. New York: Charles Scribner's Sons, 1924.

Mearns, Hughes, *Creative Youth*. New York: Garden City Publishing Co., 1925.

Moholy-Nagy, L., *The New Vision*. New York: W. W. Norton and Co., 1938.

.................., *Vision in Motion*. Chicago: P. Theobald, 1947.

Mumford, Lewis, *The Condition of Man*. New York: Harcourt, Brace and Co., 1944.

Phillips, Duncan, *The Artist Sees Differently*. New York: E. Weyhe Co., 1931.

Pope, Arthur, *Art, Artist, and Layman*. Cambridge, Mass.: Harvard University Press, 1937.

Raup, Robert, *Complacency*. New York: The Macmillan Co., 1925.

Read, Herbert, *Anatomy of Art*. New York: Dodd Mead and Co., 1932.

.................., *Art and Society*. New York: The Macmillan Co., 1937.

.................., *Education Through Art*. New York: Pantheon Books, 1945.

.................., *Grass Roots of Art*. New York: Wittenborn and Co., 1947.

Santayana, George, *The Life of Reason*. (Reason in Art.) New York: Charles Scribner's Sons, 1928.

.................., *Sense of Beauty*. New York: Charles Scribner's Sons, 1896.

Sorokin, P. A., *Social and Cultural Dynamics*. Vol. I. Fluctuations of Forms of Art. New York: American Book Co., 1937.

.................., *The Crisis of Our Age*. New York: E. P. Dutton and Co., 1945.

The Harvard Committee, *General Education in a Free Society*. Cambridge, Mass.: Harvard University Press, 1945.

Tomlinson, R. R., *Crafts for Children*. London: The Studio, 1935.

.................., *Picture Making by Children*. London: The Studio, 1934.

Ulich, Robert, *Conditions of Civilized Living*. New York: E. P. Dutton and Co., 1946.

Veblen, T., *The Theory of the Leisure Class*. New York: The Modern Library, 1934.

Whitehead, Alfred North, *Process and Reality*. New York: The Macmillan Co., 1936.

Wilenski, R. H., *The Modern Movement in Art*. London: Faber and Faber, 1932.

Index